P9-CRG-457

CAFFEINE FOR THE
CREATIVE
MIND

CAFFEINE FOR THE CREATIVE MIND

250 EXERCISES TO WAKE UP YOUR BRAIN

Stefan Mumaw & Wendy Lee Oldfield

Cincinnati, Ohio
www.howdesign.com

 Published by HOW Books, an imprint of F+W Media, Inc., 4700 East Galbraith Road, Cincinnati, Ohio 45236. (800) 289-0963. First edition.

17 16 15 14 13 12 11 10 9 8

Distributed in Canada by Fraser Direct, 100 Armstrong Avenue, Georgetown, ON, Canada L7G 5S4, Tel: (905) 877-4411. Distributed in the U.K. and Europe by David & Charles, Brunel House, Newton Abbot, Devon, TQ12 4PU, England, Tel: (+44) 1626 323200, Fax: (+44) 1626 323319, E-mail: postmaster@davidandcharles.co.uk. Distributed in Australia by Capricorn Link, P.O. Box 704, Windsor, NSW 2756 Australia, Tel: (02) 4577-3555.

Library of Congress Cataloging-in-Publication Data

Mumaw, Stefan.
Caffeine for the creative mind : 250 exercises to wake up your brain / by Stefan Mumaw and Wendy Lee Oldfield.-- 1st ed.

p. cm.
ISBN-13: 978-1-58180-867-4 (pbk. : alk. paper)
ISBN-10: 1-58180-867-4
1. Creative ability--Problems, exercises, etc. 2. Creative thinking--Problems, exercises, etc. I. Oldfield, Wendy Lee. II. Title.

BF408.M855 2006
153.3'5--dc22

2006004446

Cover and interior design by
Wendy Lee Oldfield

Editor: Amy Schell
In-house Art Director: Grace Ring
Production Coordinator: Greg Nock

Stefan Mumaw

Stefan Mumaw graduated with a BFA in graphic design from Chapman University in 1996. Since that time, he has written two books on the subject of web design (*Simple Websites* and *Redesigning Websites*), has returned to Chapman University to teach creative web design, and has become a partner and creative director at The Brainyard, a small advertising agency in Costa Mesa, CA. Stefan has been undeservedly blessed with a beautiful wife, Niqua, and a rambunctious daughter, Caitlyn. And Ed the cat.

Dedication

In life, you get few opportunities to forge friendships that you pray will last the remainder of your days here on Earth. God has blessed me with not one, but three. This book is dedicated to Rob, Umahl and Joe.

My Best Friends.

Wendy Lee Oldfield

Wendy Lee Oldfield was born in Johannesburg, South Africa, and has lived in Greece and The Netherlands. After moving to the United States and graduating with a BFA in graphic design from Chapman University in 2004, Wendy started her own part-time graphic design company, Vekay Creative. *Caffeine for the Creative Mind* is Wendy's first book. She resides in Southern California with her filmmaker boyfriend Bob. They don't have a cat.

Dedication

This book is dedicated to my greatest heroes in the world.

My Mom and Dad.

Contents

Introduction 16
Pimp My Red Flyer 20
How'd THAT Get There? 21
I Tried It ***22***
I Actually Have a Need for a Hacksaw at My Studio 23
High Fructose Corn Syrup Is Not a Banned Substance 24
This Exercise Puts So Much Pressure on Me… HEY! 25
Circular Heaven 26
I Could Have Sworn That Sign Means "Walk Stiffly" 27
Is Anyone Home? 28
Interview: Terry Marks **29**
I Think My Seven-Year-Old Could Beat Me In a Race 34
The Love Bug Returns! 35
Rock Star! 36
And Your Name Was…? 37
Bugs Just Wanna Have Fun! 38
Stupid "K" 39
That's Not the Words! 40
Danger, Will Robinson, Danger! 41
I Tried It ***42***
The Ultimate Desk 43
What Day Is It? 44
Red and Blue Dogs 45
Egg Drop Soup 46
Don't Underestimate the Power of Example! 47
Where Is That "Q" I've Been Saving? 48
Dude, C'mon! 49
The "Million Dollar Idea" List 50
Is That How They Made the Pyramids? 51
Interview: Kevin Carroll **52**
Good Fences Make Good Neighbors 62
Shhhh. I'm Hunting Wabbits 63
It's Sort of Like Volleyball, But With Joe as the Ball 64
That Guy Is the Shape of a Caslon "R," Huh? 65
My Words Caught a Fly 66
I Was Told There'd Be No Math 67
Once Upon a Tune 68
Gnome, Gnome on the Range 69

More Contents

My Astro-Toupee 70
I Tried It ***71***
No Rules! 72
Dude, Nice Koala Pinky! 73
Tick, Tick, Tick, Tick, Boom! 74
What's a "Dot-Com"? 75
I Knew He'd Have a Book of Potions, Right? 76
Sharpie; Shirt Pocket; Laundry Bill 77
Is That a Diamond-Studded Coffee Mug? 78
I Tried It ***79***
Hold On, I'm Folding My Quarter 80
Take a Seat 81
What Is That Thing Dangling From Your Other Arm? 82
Three Things 83
You Got a "D" In Font Selection? 84
Can Anyone Direct Me to the Perfume Aisle? 85
Interview: Denise Weyhrich **86**
What the Heck Is a Quince? 91
Survival of the Fittest 92
There is Always a Better Way 93
Why Can't I Have an Evil Lair, Too? 94
If You Cross Your Eyes Like That, They'll Stay That Way 95
You Want an Acme WHAT? 96
I Tried It ***97***
Where Was This 25 Years Ago? 98
Defend Yourself! 99
Agency Oz 100
Mirror, Mirror on the Desk 101
Can You Feel the Love? 102
Excuse Me, Your Three o'Clock Is Here 103
That Looks Just Like Nothing 104
I Tried It ***105***
Nice Hood Ornament! 106
Holy Nightmares, Batman! 107
White or Wheat? 108
Prehistoric Voicemail? 109
Et Tu, Rombus 3000? 110
Para-Military… Pens? 111

And More Contents

Did You Get That License? 112
I'll Take a Double Scoop of Pay-Toilet, Please 113
Can You Get Curds at the Deli Down the Street? 114
Our Janitor Doesn't Look Like That! 115
And the Pitch… TOUCHDOWN! 116
Pimp My Catapult! 117
Interview: Brian Sack **118**
I Think It Needs More (Insert Noun Here) 122
Fore! Five! Watch Out! 124
Is That a Fire Pole? 125
I'm New and Improved! 126
Did He Just Tell Me to Steal Third or Is His Nose Running? 127
How Do You Say "Red" In Caveman? 128
So Should I Stop Where I Am or Run? 129
Mmmmm… Cardboard 130
It's Even Got Flaps! 131
Don't Push That Button! 132
An "E" Ticket Ride 133
I Tried It ***134***
In a Land Far, Far Away… 135
Can Someone Show Me the Door? 136
My Totem Is Teetering 137
I'll Take the Double Raptor Meal Deal, Please 138
I Didn't Think She Could Eat All of That 139
I Can't Find the Surprise! 140
Sorry, Charlie 141
We've Got Spirit, Yes We Do! 142
I Wear My Sun-Survivor-Goggle-Glasses at Night 143
Mine Has Five Colored Rings! 144
Rest In Peace 145
Box That Ferret, Please 146
I Already Have That One! 147
Interview: Steve Morris **148**
Let's Introduce You to Alex 153
Superman's Not Home Right Now 154
Back In My Day, the Fans Didn't Have Lasers 155
How Do I Get Ink off My Desk Again? 156
How Do You Draw Music? 157
It Keeps Things Hot AND Cold! 158
I Didn't Know I Had It In Me 159

And Even More Contents

Top Dog 160
Scott "Tired of Bein'" Poe Called for You 161
Shoot, I Pulled the Door Off Again! 162
***I Tried It* 163**
Life In the Fast Lane! 164
Where's This Going? 165
That Penguin Is Throwing Up on My Pants 166
A Little Dab'll Do Ya! 167
My New Shoes Are Stuck in the ATM 168
Is This How Milton and Bradley Started? 169
And It Still Staples 170
Do These Shorts Make My Line Look Big? 171
What Time Is It? 172
Where's That Copy of Emoticons Illustrated? 173
The Pet Rock Just Got Booted 174
I'll Take the Next Catapult, Thanks 175
Interview: Mike Dietz 176
Does This Dress Make My Brain Look Fat? 181
Don't Put This on Your Hood, Though 182
Wave 'Em Proud 183
You're Fired! 184
I Wouldn't Have Chosen Relish for the Carpet, But That's Just Me 185
Where'd They Get THAT?! 186
What Does SHE Over THERE Have to Do With THAT? 187
I'm Gonna Need a Bigger Fishbowl! 188
The Envelope, Please 189
I Never Knew So Much About a Pencil Sharpener 190
What Does Melancholy Look Like? 191
We Got the Beat! 192
Black Eye Bart's a-Lookin' for Ya! 193
Poor Hamster… Never Had a Chance 194
***I Tried It* 195**
I Call It "Helveticaslon" 196
How Do You Photograph Smelly? 197
Twinkies Count as Two 198
Should Bees Wear Kneepads? 199
I Can't Come In, I Have the Gout 200
I Can't Spell "Abnormal Martian" With Just Seven Characters! 201
Like, Ummmm… I Mean, It's Like… 202
Yes, Doc, I Think I Broke My Pancreas Sleeping 203

Sheesh-More Contents

Tweety Would Freak 204
Trick or Pantone Book? 205
Is My Hair OK? 206
We're Gettin' Hitched! 207
Did You Just Get Really, Really Mad at That Bank Robber? 208
Alohamobile 209
Interview: Peleg Top **210**
Knock Knock! 215
Shoot! I Left the Ten Trophy Again! 216
Very Green 217
Drats 218
Oh No, They Didn't! 219
Does That Come In Suede? 220
I'll Have The BBQ Rack of Vader Please! 221
What an Odd Place for a Totem Pole 222
Dumb as a Rock 223
Have a Nice Day! 224
Lick and Stick 225
That's Great, Moses Is In Foul Trouble 226
Is That a Tailpipe, or Are You Just Happy to See Me? 227
Water and Air Are Cold 228
I Tried It ***229***
What's Next? 230
How Do I Make a Round Chimney? 231
Survivor: Madison Avenue 232
Oh Say Can You Peep? 233
And Then He Said... 234
What Happens From Here? 235
All Aboard! 236
Would You Like Any Fillings or Gold Caps With THAT? 237
Where'd You Get That Hot Chocolate, Dude? 238
Is That a SuperSlushee Monument Built Out of Wieners? 239
It's Good to See a Happy Potato 240
Go Joe! 241
What's That Amazing Smell? 242
Interview: Jeff Fisher **243**
I Never Knew a Pencil Sharpener Could Be So Deep 246
It's Better Than Cleaning It! 247
Is That Chest of Drawers on a Dimmer? 248
How Many Ounces of Gold Do I Need to Park Here? 249

Are You Killing Me?

Mmmm… Lincoln Logs 250
That Box Is Looking at Me 251
When Egg Noodles Die Young 252
Home Sweet Hobo Home 253
I Call Him "Upside Down Coffee Cup Man!" 254
My Guard Rail Keeps Blocking the Scanner 255
I Make a Terrible Clown 256
It Looks Like a Scribble 257
I Knew That Xylophone Would Come In Handy One Day 258
I Tried It ***259***
I Have a Full House, Marketing Directors Over Production Thugs 260
Sure Beats Hand Puppets 261
Fire In the Hole! 262
Doesn't Anyone Wear Yellow Anymore? 263
It's Up, and It's Good! 264
Haiku-a-Gogo! 265
Creatures of Habit 266
If You Want to See Your Beloved Pencil Sharpener Alive... 267
A Buffalo Would Definitely Destroy an Eagle In a Fight 268
Is That for a Dog Food Company? 269
Interview: Sayles Graphic Design **270**
HEY! She Has My Hairdo! 274
Dude, Feel Free to Pop a Mint 275
Is It a Star? 276
Mini-It! 277
How Do You Sell "And?" 278
I Tried It ***279***
I Changed That… I Think 280
We Have So Much In Common! 281
I Knew I Should Have Saved That Copy of Ice Fishing Illustrated 282
Does This Color Go With My Work Boots? 283
How Do You Get Your Lips Way Up There? 284
Big Brother Is Not Only Watching, He's Brewing Cups of Coffee for You! 285
How About Dessert? 286
I Tried It ***287***
Is That Hairnet Real? 288
Debate This! 289
EXTRA, EXTRA! Read All About It! 290
Is That a Paisley Screensaver? 291
The Wright Bros. Would Be Proud! 292

OK, Exactly How Long IS This Book?

Balder-what? 293
Interview: John Foster **294**
Hi, I'm Fido 298
Cool Vanishing Point! 299
One Meeelyun Daaaahhllers! 300
I'm Flippin' Sweet! 301
Retreat! Retreat! 302
I Don't Think They Make a Slushee That Big 303
I Tried It ***304***
Tag, You're It! 305
Did That Guy Just Say "Shucks?" 306
Wanna Play Some Mini Desk Volleyball? 307
Have You Ever Noticed That Before? 308
Desks Ahoy! 309
For Sale 310
Pablo Is Calling! 311
I Can't Hear You, I'm Screaming 312
How Could I Live Without My Combination Hot Dog Cooker and Bun Warmer? 313
Was That Jeff or Did a Car Just Backfire? 314
Where'd the Cork Go? 315
Play Ball! 316
You Mean There Really Is Truth In Advertising? 317
3, 2, 1, Score!!! 318
G.I. ...Douglas? 320
Interview: Von Glitschka **321**
Batteries Not Included 325
Ah, Go Fly a Kite 326
Bland No Longer 327
How Big Is a Bread Basket? 328
I Can't Find "Downsizing" 329
Go Fighting Brain Men! 330
My Business Helmet Keeps Falling Over My Eyes 331
You're Walking on My Line 332
Do I Use Ballpoint or Felt Tip on the Inside of My Eyelids? 333
Bachelor Number Three... 334
I Think That Florist Is a Total "H" 335
I'm for It... Wait... I Mean, I'm Against It 336
Are Mom's Cookies an "X" or an "O"? 337
Blind Man's Bluff 338
Coca-Cowpie? 339

I Give Up

Doodles from Interviewees 340
Index of Exercises by Type 352
Contributor List 359

Introduction

"Ideas are the real currency in our business. Without a good idea, all the artistic proficiency in the world is just window dressing." —Mike Dietz, Slappy Pictures

Mike uses a key word in that statement, and it's not the word you think. Mike uses the word "our." Mike Dietz is an accomplished illustrator and an equally talented animator. So who is he speaking to when he says "our" business? Simply put, he's talking to you.

You are a creative. **"What's a creative?"** you ask. In its purest form, a "creative" is anyone who creates. Anything. If you make something, you are a creative. If nothing existed, and then you appeared, and then something existed, chances are you created it. Or you're a magician. Or a witch, in which case we'd have to weigh you against a duck to be sure, but that's for another day.

While you might not describe yourself as creative, the fact is, you are. **Everyone on the planet is creative.** The only thing that differentiates those-we-think-are-truly-creative from us is execution. We all generate ideas, but few act upon those ideas, share those ideas, realize those ideas or execute those ideas. Everyone has them, but not everyone announces them. What keeps people from communicating their ideas? Mostly fear. We're all afraid that if we share our ideas, we will be rebuked by others. It's natural. But we'll never see a single idea realized until we are willing to share those ideas.

For those who make a living generating and executing ideas, sharing those ideas is part of the game. For those in the industry most commonly categorized as "the creative arts," ***idea generation is paramount to success.*** *Mike is right: Ideas are our currency. They're what we sell. Whether we're a designer, a painter, a writer, a photographer, an illustrator… ideas are what we need because ideas are what we are paid to provide. Everything else is "window dressing." The question is… "Where do we find ideas?"*

The answer is in yourself. You generate ideas. And it's difficult. But how do you get better at idea generation? Simply put, you train for it. If you were going to run a marathon in two months, you would prepare, wouldn't you? You would train for that event; you would set a schedule of activities that would prepare your body for what would be asked of it on that day, because you knew that day would arrive. What if you had to prepare for a marathon, but you didn't know what day it would start? All you knew was that it was coming. It could be any day. You would probably prepare your body every day for the chance that it might be the next day. Preparing our bodies to endure physical activity is just like preparing our minds for creative activity. Yet, we often don't take steps to effectively train for idea generation. What would happen if we didn't train for that any-day marathon? What if we just went about our regular business every day, wolfing down burritos like they were endangered, and when the day came, we straddled up to the starting line and started running. That's right… pulled hammy. Maybe two. Sometimes even three, and we only HAVE two, that's how bad it would be.

Chances are, we'd crash and burn.
The same goes for idea generation. We are often asked, in the middle of the day and with a dozen other things going on, to be creative, to generate ideas. We naturally struggle, because we haven't prepared to think creatively.

That's the very purpose of this book, to help you prepare and train to create ideas in greater quality and quantity. *In this book you will find 250 exercises that will train you to think alternatively. They will help you see things from a different perspective.* ***Creativity lurks in the vision of a slightly skewed perspective.*** *The exercises in this book will help you stretch your creativity, prepare you for greater creative thought and train you to extract ideas when you need to.*

Here's your challenge: Do one exercise every day. The exercises are short, maybe 15-20 minutes each. They are fun, they make you think, and they promote active, creative, idea generation. We encourage you to find someone to do the exercises with, someone with whom you can share the fruits of your creative ideas. You'll not only enjoy the exercises more, but you'll prepare yourself for another important aspect of idea generation, sharing the idea.
Think of it as daily creative maintenance.

This book contains six different kinds of creative exercises: design, writing, photography, problem solving, idea kindling and play. One of the best characteristics of the creative process is that it is medium-independent. You will find creative opportunities in each category, regardless of your preferred medium. Frankly, getting out of your **"comfort zone"** creatively will often lead to some of your most creative solutions!

Stretch yourself every day, don't take the easy way out, and share your ideas with someone else. You'll be better prepared for idea generation, and your creative wallet will be bulging with the currency of our industry in no time!

Pimp My Red Flyer

MTV has a ton of original programming these days. One of these successful shows is called "Pimp My Ride," where the hosts take an otherwise ordinary vehicle and "pimp it out" by re-engineering it to create a luxurious, often urban-inspired mobile transit device. Complete with all the fixin's, these new vehicles keep some characteristics of the original, and in most cases, the result is quite extraordinary. Although some of the original vehicles are rather run-down and plain, none are as simple as, say, a common red wagon. Your task today is to "Pimp My Wagon." Take an ordinary red wagon, a simple toy that most children love, and "pimp it out" with whatever luxuries and additions you can think of. Create your ultimate urban-inspired, pimped-out wagon.

Sweeeeet!

How'd THAT Get There?

We get accustomed to things being in their place. If we need to cut something, we know where the scissors are. If we need a pen, we know where to look. It's frustrating when things aren't where they are supposed to be. Sometimes we come across those items even before we are looking for them. There they are, where they don't belong. Your task today is to document those things on camera. Grab a digital camera and take ten pictures of ten things in your environment that don't belong where they are. That way, when you need them next, you'll have proof of exactly where they are! Then again, you could just put them where they should be, but that's too easy.

I TRIED IT

"This exercise caught my eye and my interest because it is so visual, and so ripe for wacky interpretation. ***It made me truly examine what tools I use to do the work I do.*** And, it turns out that the tools that live in my office make up only a minority of the gadgets, implements, utensils and machines that help me get the job done.

I had a great time brainstorming the list of features included in my extremely accommodating army knife. Ultimately, I could show only a few of the handy fold-out gadgets... The rest are still tucked inside, and include (but are not limited to): computer mouse, bottle of water, dictionary, inkwell, scanner, brain, thesaurus, tape, dog biscuits, remote control, digital camera, roll of quarters, charger, kaleidoscope, scissors, spray adhesive, a towel, and a carrot.

What an excellent exercise for reminding you that not only your inspiration, but your tools and methods as well, should be drawn from all aspects of the world around you.

I recommend a nice end-of-day cocktail to accompany this exercise—the carrot probably wouldn't be in there without it."

I Actually Have a Need for a Hacksaw at My Studio

Jessica Southwick, Old Saybrook, CT

Most of us are familiar with the Swiss Army Knife, that clever gadget that houses 276 tools in one handy red plastic sheath. **As creatives, we may never have a glaring need for a 2" hack saw,** but there are things that we use every day in our professional lives that might make more useful tools. Your task is to invent your "Professional Survival Swiss Army... Thing." What would YOUR sheathed utility tool hold? Draw it on a piece of paper, or simply list the items it would have.

High Fructose Corn Syrup Is Not a Banned Substance

We drink 'em all day, and regardless of our personal stance on recycling, the containers are rarely used for anything besides filling up a receptacle. That's going to change, at least for today. So down that carbonated beverage of yours, and get crackin'! Your challenge today is to get two other willing participants and race those cans! **Create a vehicle out of an empty soda can.** It can be land-based if you have an incline to roll down, water-based if there is a body of water handy, or even air-based if you can engineer a way to keep it airborne long enough to judge distance. Use whatever elements you have at your disposal to create the way it will roll, float or fly. You can even decorate it with sponsor logos or speed aides. The sky's the limit, or the wall at the end of the hall, whichever comes first.

This Exercise Puts So Much Pressure on Me... HEY!

Create a pictogram that describes each of these six words: **Pressure, Delirious, Lucky, Suspense, Dangerous and Joyful**. *Use only four straight lines and a circle for each one. You can arrange the lines and the circle in whatever fashion you desire, but you can only use four lines and one circle. The lines must be of equal length and not divided in any way, and the circle must be kept whole.*

Denise Weyrich, Orange, CA

Circular Heaven

Don't get *dizzy*, here! We're going to go photo-exploring a little today. Get your digital camera. Today's task is to take twenty pictures of twenty different circles. The caveat is that you have to frame the circle in the same place in the photograph each time you take one. Explore your immediate area first, then move onto other areas, even go outside if need be. Find twenty things that make a circle, and take the photos so that the circle takes up the same amount of space and is framed the same way from picture to picture.

I Could Have Sworn That Sign Means "Walk Stiffly"

If we took one class in drivers education, we're aware of what each of the common road signs mean. If it's yellow with a curved arrow pointing right, we know there's a curve coming up to the right. But what if we didn't know what they meant? Some of those signs might be communicating more than the designers bargained for. Your task today is to come up with alternate meanings for the following five common roadsigns:

Is Anyone Home?

What if? Imagine for a moment this what if: No electricity in your office. None. How would you communicate to your coworkers if there were no e-mail, no phone, no IM? Obviously, you'd be forced to get up and go over to their office, but what if you couldn't? What if you worked at an office that chained you to your desk by your ankles, with one of those giant iron balls on the other end of the chain? Could happen. How would you communicate then? Gotcha. But how long can you yell without losing your voice? Your task today is to live in this imaginary world for a moment. Create a communication system that your office could use in this scenario. Consider how you'd rig it up, how messages would pass back and forth, etc.

Seriously, stop yelling!

interview
with
TERRY
MARKS

We've all met people like Terry Marks. And unilaterally... we loathe them. They represent all that is good and decent and talented in this world, all the things we are not but aspire to be. Terry is a creative director, a designer, an illustrator, a film maker, a studio head, an AIGA board member, a speaker, a teacher and a humanitarian. But most of all, **Terry would want to be known as a storyteller.** For in storytelling, "people are inspired."

Among the buckets full of accolades Terry's Seattle-based agency, tmarks, has received, none mean as much to Terry as the ones that put his charitable work in focus within the community. ***tmarks has a history of taking on some projects that paid little, but gave much.*** This philosophy has not only given Terry and his team an opportunity to do some good in the community, but an opportunity to s t r e t c h both their creative muscle as well as their heart muscle. "Anybody that does creative work for a non-profit or comes up with an idea that's just a good idea," Terry starts, "they want it out there so that people can make use of it. ***They realize there's a need and understand they're not going to get any money or accolades or recognition out of it.*** Everybody here wants to work on that kind of project. We've always tried to provide a space if you're one of our designers to do stuff like that. To do a project where you get to infuse more of your soul into something changes the way you look at your entire job."

One would think assembling that kind of team would be difficult, putting together a group of talented, caring, thoughtful creatives that can bring something unique to the firm. Indeed, it seems Terry has a unique approach to hiring. "People always say 'do you hire for skill or personality?'" Terry reports. "Actually, neither! Skills can be learned if they have the aptitude, and some people can have a great personality and don't know how to work. So what I've always responded with is that **we hire for soul.** The core stuff. We have to care about the same things, because when you're working in a small company, someone can pee in the pool so fast. And as a studio head, you have to manage that. It's creating an environment that is rewarding, that feels like you're doing something beneficial."

Doing rewarding, beneficial work would be fruitless if the work didn't meet the creative challenge. Terry's inherent desire to find creative solutions has given him the opportunity to do some fantastic, award-winning design work. "Fostering a creative environment is so important," Terry says. "I would hope that I lead a little bit in that pursuit here. I've done everything from making movies to sculpting characters—stuff that has nothing to do with the corporate world—just because I need to make stuff. **I think that people that are creative are that way because they can't help it.** You don't know you're creative when you're a little kid when you're making all this stuff—you're just doing what comes naturally."

"For example, there's this program that we do with high school kids where we do nine workshops a year. There's a couple of kids who will go out and just do a photo safari. We'll go down to a market and shoot photos for the afternoon and go get our film developed and compare. I just think that stuff is so important.

We have a few come back once or twice a month with something like, 'this is a story I wrote' or 'this is a photo I took' or 'this is a piece of art I made.' It doesn't have a lot to do with design, but it does something creative. And I think that, as a studio head, it's vital to encourage your team to expand the same way because the best creativity for design or one discipline usually comes from outside that discipline. It's your experience that informs it uniquely. Otherwise it's just design recycling design."

It also seems like Terry is a believer in the creatively-rejuvenating effects of play. "We have our bowling night, or we've flown to Disneyland for the day as a surprise, and then came back the same night. One time we closed the office at noon, went and checked in at the W Hotel, went out for an afternoon movie, cleaned up, went out for a big dinner at the restaurant, went out salsa dancing, and then everyone was in my room watching movies all night. But we had to be back at work the next day. It was like 24-hour vacation!"

Yep, it's official. We loathe him.

Terry Marks, tmarks Design, www.tmarksdesign.com

Rock Star!

While we may never be on stage in front of thousands of screaming fans, there's still

a rock star in all of us!

We just need the right instrument. It's time we made one. Look around your current environment and find five things you can use to make an instrument.

It can be percussion, strings, wind… the sky's the limit. **Figure out how the elements you've found would be assembled together if you had to go on stage in front of thousands of screaming fans and play it live!**

Rock on!

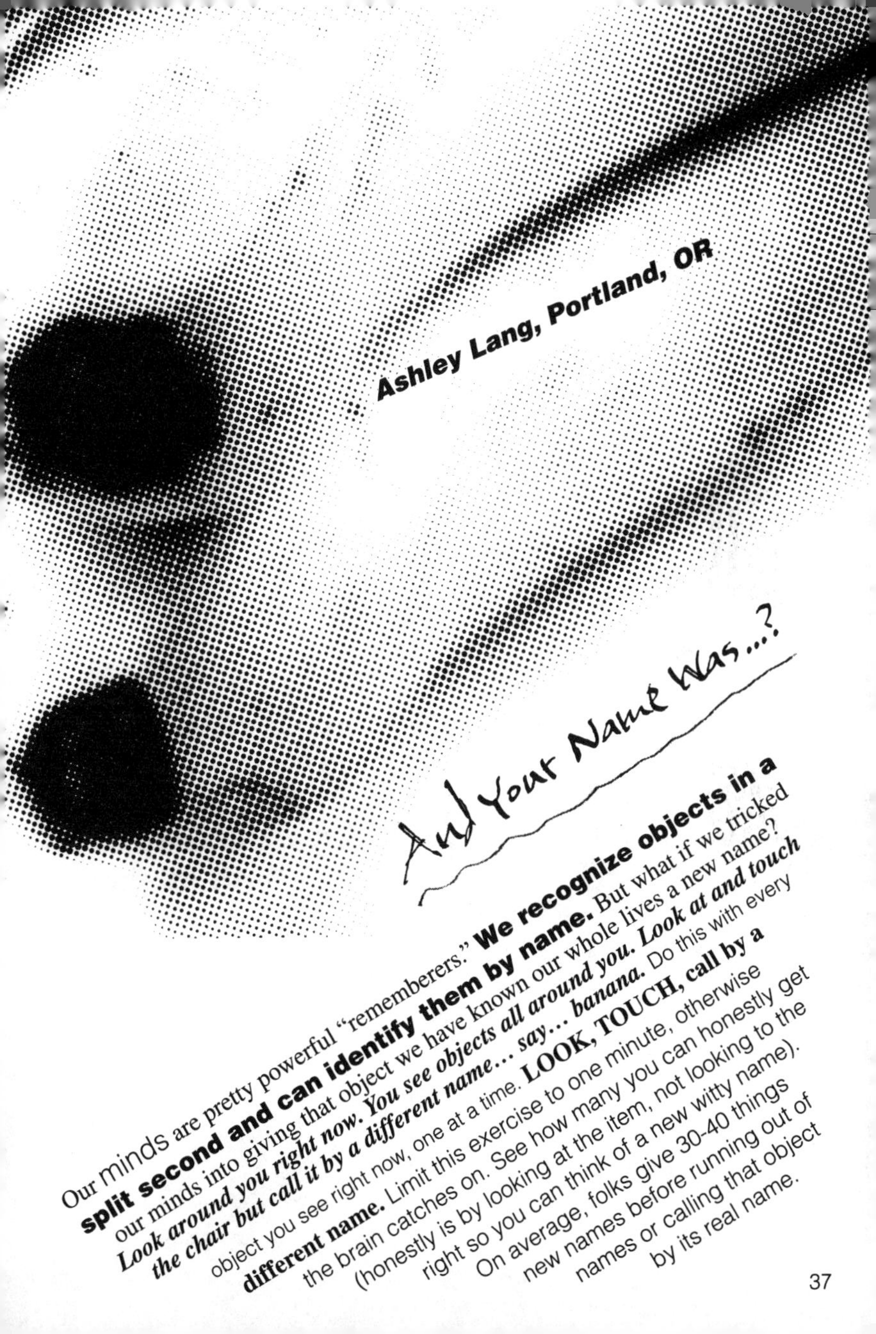

Ashley Lang, Portland, OR

And Your Name Was...?

Our minds are pretty powerful "rememberers." **We recognize objects in a split second and can identify them by name.** But what if we tricked our minds into giving that object we have known our whole lives a new name? ***Look around you right now. You see objects all around you. Look at and touch the chair but call it by a different name… say… banana.*** Do this with every object you see right now, one at a time. **LOOK, TOUCH, call by a different name.** Limit this exercise to one minute, otherwise the brain catches on. See how many you can honestly get (honestly is by looking at the item, not looking to the right so you can think of a new witty name). On average, folks give 30-40 things new names before running out of names or calling that object by its real name.

Bugs Just Wanna Have Fun!

Is it their fault they're the size of… well, an ant? Bugs deserve to experience the *thrill* of s p e e d and gravity without the fear of ending up on the bad side of someone's front bumper. And you're just the creative to give it to them! Your task is to design a c a r n i v a l r i d e for a bug. But you can only use the materials you have in your immediate area to make it. **You can disassemble objects to use various parts, utilize your environment, or even find ways to include the natural elements in your current space as propellants!**

Stupid "K"

Numbers and letters are beautiful artistic forms on their own merit, *but we have difficulty seeing them as anything but what they truly mean. We often don't see the beauty in the form.* Only after turning the letters inside and out, or flipping the numbers over, can we truly appreciate their design. Your task today is to do just that. This will be easiest on the computer, but can be done on paper as well. Type or write your full name. Your task is to recreate your full name using letters and numbers. The only rule is you can't use the actual letter. So if your name starts with an ***S***, you can use any form of any other letter or number, backwards or forwards, upside down or right side up–except an actual ***S***.

That's Not The Words!

We remember music. It seems every other important piece of cerebral information we need to retain is lost at the most inopportune moment while that song playing on the alarm clock when we woke up is stuck in our heads indefinitely. It's time to put that infernal tune to good use. ***Look around you right now and choose a person or object.*** Now take the melody in your head (if one is strangely absent at this moment, turn on the radio and find a song you know) and change the chorus of the song to be about that person or object.

Write your new lyrics on a piece of paper. If that song won't leave your troubled mind, write a new verse. ***If you're feeling saucy, write each verse to the song as the day progresses until the song is completely re-written. Now stand on your chair and sing it out loud!***

(embarrassing moment optional)

Danger, Will Robinson, Danger!

Science fiction has been predicting the rise of the robot for decades. Although robots are an active part of our technological culture, most of us don't actually own one. Until now. Your task is to build the shell of a robot out of the objects you see around you right now. It obviously won't work, but that's ITs problem! It can be in the shape of a human, animal, or even some futuristic space creature!

"I gave the Ultimate Desk exercise to my Art 396 Junior Seminar in Graphic Design class. It was interesting to note that the students came in somewhat lethargic right after lunch. The exercise was read and they went to work. The mood of the design students changed; there was lots of laughing, sketching, writing. They really seemed to experience an attitude change and an energy boost. They especially enjoyed sharing with their classmates the desk they designed.

(he tried it!!)

I'm convinced that creativity is directly linked to mood. A good mood leads to a good attitude and that leads to creativity."

Eric Chimenti

Tustin, CA

The Ultimate Desk

Our desks usually are purchased from a pre-determined template, meaning we have little say in the design and function of them. What if we did? What if we had an unlimited budget and complete access to a team of engineers and craftsmen that could build our Ultimate Desk? What would we add or subtract?

That is your task: to design your ultimate desk. Consider shape, depth, and function. Take into account factors such as power or shelving, and computer-related needs. Draw it out on a piece of paper as if you have to communicate your ideas to the engineering team.

What Day Is It?

The week of seven days was adopted in Rome somewhere about 400 AD and spread into Europe, but it had been recognized long before that in the East. The names of each of the days are generally associated with Roman mythology. It's time they received an updated, contemporary change. Your task is to rename the days of the week to be more modern. They can all be associated with a theme, or they can all have different meanings. They can be as long or as short as you like, but they all must end with the suffix "-day," like they do now.

Red and Blue Dogs

Professional sports leagues all seem to share similar graphic qualities in their logos. There are typically two or three colors and a negative space shape representing a player or a recognizable object from the game. Your task is to design a professional sports league logo for these five activities:

Hot Dog Eating
Kite Flying
Tricycle Racing
Painting
Car Washing

Egg Drop Soup

You must create a container for an egg that will safely keep the egg from breaking when dropped from a two-story window. The container can be made of whatever materials you deem appropriate. Draw a sketch of the container as if you were going to show a craftsmen what your idea is and how to make it. Use a dotted line to signify where the egg would be, inside of the container, and callouts to describe what the materials are and what their functions would be.

Don't Underestimate The Power of Example!

Showing someone how to do something is the easiest form of communication. But as communicators, we rarely get that level of intimacy with our target audience, so we must use other methods to reach our intended market. Sometimes, the most difficult form of communication is using words.

Time to get back to basics! On a piece of paper, write out, in words only, instructions on how to tie a shoelace.

Kate Dow, Des Moines, IA

Where Is That "Q" I've Been Saving?

How well do you know your own personal workspace? You're about to find out! Using a digital camera, take a picture of each letter of the alphabet on things ONLY in your current space. Each letter MUST be from a different object. You can move objects to reveal lettering, or maybe even to create lettering!

Denise Weyhrich, Orange, CA

Dude, C'mon!

You'll need another willing participant for this exercise. Have your friend draw a squiggle on a piece of paper. The crazier the better. Your friend then gets to define the "category" (like sports, weather, or toys) and your task is to create something in that category from that squiggle. When you've done so, it's your turn to create the squiggle and category for your friend.

Jonathon Redman, Roachdale, IN

The "Million Dollar Idea" List

We keep one at the studio. We've been adding to it for the last ten years, everything from practical ideas to absurd revelations. The Million Dollar Idea List is exactly that: ***a list of ideas of things that would potentially make us a million dollars if we ever really produced them.*** We've seen ideas from our list actually produced and someone made a million dollars... just not one of us. We've even started keeping a "Someone Stole Our Million Dollar Idea" list. It's time you start your own. Everyone has an idea for a product or improvement that could make a million dollars if ever produced. What's yours? Start with yours, then walk around your current environment and ask others for their additions to the list. Who knows, you might actually make a million someday! (Our best idea was to sell our list, by the way. You can't use that!)

Mike MacLane and some friends of Russ Rohrer, Costa Mesa, CA

Is That How They Made the Pyramids?

Point of view can make the difference between good and great. **By looking at problems from another point of view, we can often find solutions that we've never seen before.** *Putting yourself in the shoes of another, figuratively speaking of course, often provides an alternate view. On a piece of paper, draw nine triangles, all of equal size and composition and equally spaced across the entire paper. Now, interpret those triangles from another's point of view by completing a drawing using the triangles. Create something out of each triangle that sees it from the point of view of:*

1) A Mad Scientist
2) A Baseball Player
3) A Dancer
4) A School Bus Driver
5) A Mortician
6) A Street Cart Hot Dog Vendor
7) A Fish
8) A Lawyer
9) A Zookeeper

— INTERVIEW WITH —

Kevin Carroll

Kevin Carroll is the founder of The Katalyst Consultancy and the author of ***Rules of the Red Rubber Ball: Find and Sustain Your Life's Work***, published by ESPN Books. If you don't own this book, immediately go to your local online bookseller and buy it. Right now. Go ahead, we'll wait. It's that important…

Ok, you're back. Did you read it? *Rules of the Red Rubber Ball* should be every creative's rallying cry. The concepts and stories laid out in the small but powerful edition are both life-changing and familiar. **Kevin writes of "play" and the importance of play in our lives**. Kevin has done it all: military service, collegiate and professional sports medicine, Creative Katalyst for Nike and now author and speaker. Kevin has seen his share of corporate environments, and he's spoken to his share of people that could use a little play in their lives. Especially those searching for that elusive component of idea generation: creativity.

"Creativity, to me," Carroll begins, "is the ability to have the eyes of a child—eyes of wonder, eyes of possibility—throughout your entire life. And then be able to use that creative insight or vision or ability to see things, to solve problems or to affect something for a more positive outcome. It has to do with getting inside and around an idea or a problem where someone didn't see that possibility, and many times it's not a matter of it being some monumental "ah-hah!" moment. **It could be one degree of change in something, because of a shift of the light that's shining on it, or maybe the weather has some effect on the color. What makes a change in a very dramatic way for you could simply be a slight alteration of perspective.** When we look at things through the eyes that we all had when we were children, then we have the ability to see things with the eyes of possibility and the eyes of wonder, eyes of first. ***When we were children, everything was a first. Basically, we saw things for the first time–and that's a wonderful mask of experience."***

Creativity has become the persona of many brands these days, brands that have recognized that creativity is attractive and it sells. Nike has become a leader in this direction, in part, due to the work of Nike Katalyst and Master Storyteller, Kevin Carroll. "At Nike, I felt my job had two distinct parts. The 'katalyst' part was to remind everyone of their creativity capacity and that everybody has the ability to bring creative thought to work, regardless of the position, title, or discipline you are working in at the company. So I tried to create the opportunity for everyone to have a point of view as it relates to the creative process. Everyone has playable time around an idea, so it doesn't matter if you are in strategic planning or finance or legal or design or advertising or marketing… Everyone has to be able to understand an idea and its effect, or the impact that it could have on the business, and if everyone didn't understand the idea or didn't see how they could help to foster or drive an idea with their business discipline or area, then I failed. I really tried to build a bridge between the functional areas of the company and the creative areas of the company and to get a more integrated effort around idea generation and ideation that was happening in the company. ***For instance, I would have someone from strategic planning or finance or legal come to a design brief and sit at the back of the room and be a fly on the wall and take notes, but they wouldn't have to interject anything –they would just be taking in the information and recognizing down the road that this thing's going to come across their desk.*** *With that, we also created early advocates throughout the company for an idea.* ***We as human beings love to feel included. If we don't feel included we cross our arms and say*** 'he better convince me.' ***We become advocates for an idea if we feel included in it."***

"The 'master storyteller' part of my job was really speaking to people about the power of story as it relates to our own story. Everybody brings a story of WHY to the workplace–of who I am and why I'm here. I also tried to get people to recognize their personal vision, what it is that they're bringing here. I would tell people, 'I hope that you recognize and really share the vision of this brand because if not, then you're counter-productive. Even though you think you're doing your job well, you're not fully invested.' I just tried to get people to understand first and foremost their own story, then understand the brand story. Both work together in a cool and powerful and meaningful way."

While at Nike, Kevin was charged with building an environment to help encourage a more playful, creative mindset. "I helped build a creativity rehab center–it's almost like a creativity gym, if you will, where individuals could come in and sign up for creative boosting programs. These ranged from sending people on an immersion opportunity trip to providing different training vehicles or tools to use. We provided everything from articles to magazines to books to videos about creativity and innovation and idea generation. They could look at peformance DVDs like *Stomp*, or a DVD called *Why Man Creates* by Saul Bass, or read an article from industry rags like *HOW* magazine or *Communication Arts*. I was constantly curating that and actually making a museum of creativity and creative boosting materials. It really was a multi-sensory experience. It never was about 'Oh! Well now you're ready to come up with the big ideas,' it was always about having more creative constants, more creative stamina. ***You need that kind of energy and stamina to always be able to push through when others get tired.*** When you're going through ideation, you actually have the ***energy*** and stamina and capacity to continue to push through the problem. People, just like athletes, will perform better if they have a heightened sense of confidence. They can say 'I've prepared myself that much better for the game,' and so it is for creatives and for people that have to just come up with solutions for their business. Many times the arena is business and the game is product generation, revenue generation, and increasing profits for your company–that's the game. How do you come to that with more confidence? By doing this work. It's by doing this extra work. By putting in this extra time–just like an athlete does. The athlete has obviously been conditioning with pre-season work, studying the game plan, learning what the competition is doing, and yet it's just that piece that we don't look at.

Creativity is a muscle.

We often don't look at it in terms of something that can be trained, but it can be trained. And I think that we did it naturally as children because we had to discover our world. Once we felt as if we'd discovered enough, we didn't really keep working at it, but there's always that opportunity to continue to grow and learn each and every day. **Therein lies the biggest opportunity—to recognize that you're in life-long learning mode."**

Kevin speaks often about redeveloping a child-like view of the world, because he truly believes that this perspective leads to a greater awareness of our surroundings and will, in turn, allow us to develop more ideas through more experience. Along with this perspective, Kevin is a huge advocate of play. "I recently talked with a gentleman from a huge information technology company and he said to me, 'You recently spoke to our company, and it was good to hear your philosophy, because we completely agree with the concept of play, but our leadership team couldn't see the value, and literally chastised us for playing at all.

Well, things shifted and **that leadership was taken out of position because productivity went down,** morale went down. And the new leadership came in and promoted 'fun' and 'play.' They had all these different areas that they designated 'play areas' in the company. They found an empty room and they had these two hockey tournaments. Magically, productivity went up again, morale went up again, the camaraderie, the inventiveness. It's all found in those things we were doing. ***You spoke of the importance of play within the workplace–and we completely understood because we knew what it did for us as far as freeing our minds to solve***

these problems after you had a chance to play.' You see, play is not always frivolous. There is strategic play. In the midst of play there has to be this inventiveness, there has to be this problem solver, there has to be this abstract thinker, there has to be this creative person, there has to be this amazing ability to be able to take risk, which are all the things which we are asked to do in a business setting. It's re-awakening new areas in you, and I think there are so many ways to really address play in a manner where it's comfortable for adults… so it's not just always about rolling out toys and games. There is a message and a meaning and a direction behind it, so you can put certain toys out that are all about abstract thinking. **You can put certain toys out that are all about inventing something.** You can put out something that is designed to challenge you to come up with a resolution to a conflict.

I recently read research results about Nobel laureates. One hundred and fifty Nobel laureates

were interviewed, and they found that every single one of them had an application or a hobby that they were as equally passionate about as their work.

And every single one of them said that most of their ideas came when they were doing their hobby or their application. If those guys have figured it out and recognized the value of finding something joyful and playful and keeping it around, why isn't it good enough for the rest of us?"

And what advice would he give creatives and studio heads alike? "For creatives, evaluate the environment that you're being asked to come up with ideas in. That environment might be stifling and challenging for you and maybe you just need to change your perspective. Even when you're in these 'amazing' creative spaces, it's still your normal daily place that you go and it still can become white noise, so find that time each and every day to get out of your normal environment and to get

outside your comfort zone, outside your normal area.

For studio heads, always build into your budget a chance for people to go and experience something that will feed their creative souls. Make sure that you never compromise that from your budget, and that it's always available for people to get at least one opportunity to be fed. Be strategic about this sort of trip, too. If it's to go to an industry conference, then go to that and also hit the theater and see a play, or go to a concert or hit the museums. Create a way to use that trip to see a variety of things, even project-related things, like going to see a client. You're going to get a multisensory experience as part of the immersion. Be sure to keep them accountable and ask them to share the story, share the information, share the value, share the outcome. There's this wonderful opportunity for you to go and be recreational, but there's also a responsibility. So R+R sort of shifts a little bit so it's recreational, but it's also a responsibility for you to come back with some information of value to share with the rest of us. Don't compromise on that budget and make sure that people get a chance to get out and be fed because they're always going to need ***nutrition for their creative soul.***"

Kevin Carroll, The Katalyst Consultancy, www.katalystconsultancy.com

Now go play something!

Good Fences Make Good Neighbors.

Barriers keep things out... or in, depending on your point of view. We create barriers to protect what's ours. Strangely, that is true for both physical AND mental barriers. **We put up fences in our minds to protect us from embarrassment, pain or trouble.** Both physically and mentally, barriers are all around us. While some are meant to protect, others simply keep us from accomplishing the greatness we deserve to achieve. But before we can differentiate the two, we have to identify them. Grab a digital camera. Your task today is to take fifteen pictures of barriers. They can be physical barriers, things that divide or surround, or they can represent mental barriers of some kind. Take pictures of the barriers, print them out, then examine them in your life. Do they protect or inhibit?

The eternal question!

Shhh. I'm Hunting wabbits

Secretly, you've done it all your life. A target presents itself, and you, armed with only your trusty sidekick, the rubber band, take aim. As the target moves into sight, you take aim, steady with the confidence of numerous years of rubber band training. As you release the band, you duck back inside your shelter, waiting to hear the sound of victory…

OUCH!!

Bullseye! Grab a friend and a target. (Preferably stationary and not alive!) It's time to see whose years of training have paid off. Five shots each from your own pre-defined distance. Closest to the bullseye wins.

It's Sort of Like Volleyball, But with Joe as the Ball

Sports are ingrained into our psyches as youngsters. We love sports. We would play all day if the sun would always stay in the sky. Alas, now we are confined to our desks, sentenced to only play sports at lunch and on weekends. But what if we could play a sport right now!? What would we use as equipment? **What are the rules?** That's your task right now, to create a new sport, playable right there in your office or studio, using only the things you have available to you right now. Look around you. Write down all the rules. Then,

GO PLAY IT!

That Guy Is the Shape of a Caslon "R," Huh?

How many magazines have we thumbed through in our lifetime? From articles to editorials to ads, we see a lot of media in these magazines. We often find great photography, thumbing through magazines. Photography that is so well lit, so well composed, that we simply enjoy taking it wholly in. Great photography is an art, as is great typography. Type, in its shape and composition, often takes on a personification; it becomes lifelike. Let's see just how similar these two artforms can be. This is a two-part task. First, thumb through a magazine and find a photo you like, preferably full page. Examine the composition, the shape of the items, the layout of the elements. Scan that photo. Now the fun begins. The second part of this task is to find a single letter form, a single character of type that best represents that photograph. Consider all of the same elements: shape, composition, form. Look for the typography version of your photo in a single character.

My Words Caught a Fly

Look around your current space and identify a random company name. Write that name on the center of a piece of paper and circle the name. Draw six lines from that circle. At the end of each line, write a word that is related to the word in the circle. Now, draw another six lines from each of these words and continue the process until you have four "expansions." Take a word from the outer web and try to tie it to the word in the center of the web. This is a great **brainstorming** tool when looking for ***alternative views*** for a project or client.

Laura Barnes, Cary, NC

I Was Told There'd Be No Math

Ever wonder where numbers came from? OK, maybe not, but there is some mystery to these magic characters. Ever wonder how we would count if there were no numbers? OK, again, maybe not. There is a lot of security in numbers. They never lie. There are no double meanings. There's no past tense, present tense, participles or conjunctions. There are only ten useable digits, and every number is made up of some collection of them. Then there are things like Roman numerals, an alternate system of numbers. In the vein of Roman numerals, your task today is to create a new set of "numbers." Your only restriction is that they can't be numbers, and they can't be Roman numerals. Invent another writable, countable method for representing numbers.

Once Upon a Tune

Alan Jardine, an original founding member of The Beach Boys, and illustrator Jimmy Pickering took the classic Beach Boys tune Sloop John B and made it into a children's book called Sloop John B: A Pirate's Tale. The story slightly strays from the song, but stays in perfect harmony with the original timing and lyrics of the folk tune. Your task today is to do the same thing, but with the song of your choice. Choose a song and make a children's story out of it. Don't get caught up with finding the perfect song. It can be any song, and doesn't necessarily have to use the lyrics word for word, but must stay relatively true to the overall song. If you're really feeling spicy, consider drawing the pages to go with it!

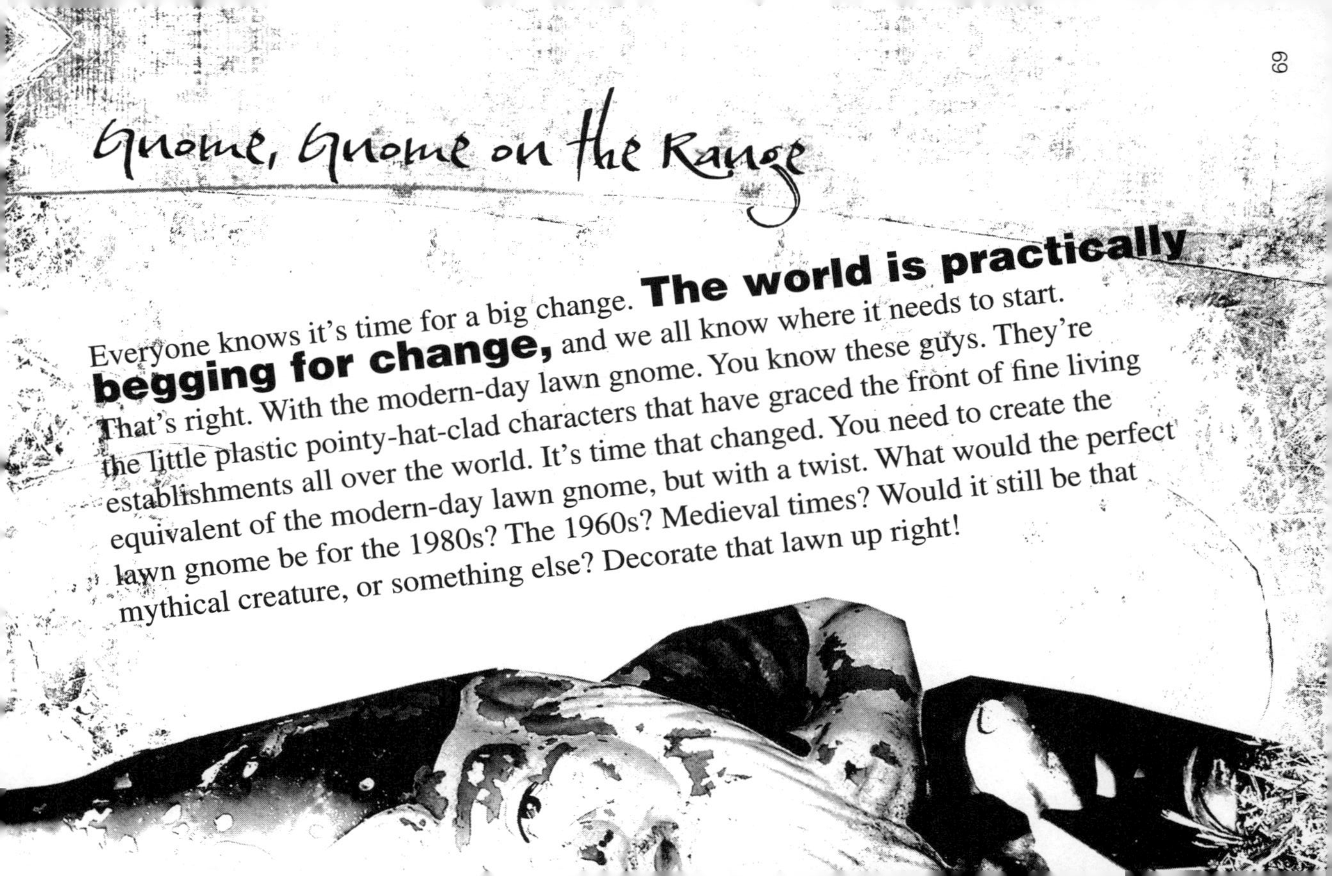

Gnome, Gnome on the Range

Everyone knows it's time for a big change. **The world is practically begging for change,** and we all know where it needs to start. That's right. With the modern-day lawn gnome. You know these guys. They're the little plastic pointy-hat-clad characters that have graced the front of fine living establishments all over the world. It's time that changed. You need to create the equivalent of the modern-day lawn gnome, but with a twist. What would the perfect lawn gnome be for the 1980s? The 1960s? Medieval times? Would it still be that mythical creature, or something else? Decorate that lawn up right!

My Astro-Toupee

Most of us have hair on our heads. (And for those who don't, this may be really fun!) Now is your chance to be different and stand out from the rest of us. Instead of hair on your head, write down five alternatives that could adorn that gorgeous head of yours. It can be anything from food to metal–this is your chance to ***dream up something wild!*** Now, take your favorite idea from the list and sketch it out as if you are describing it to a friend. It doesn't have to be a work of art, just enough to get the idea across.

Sharon Figel, East Windsor, NJ

I TRIED IT!

"This exercise was so much fun to draw. My head looked kind of stupid, but really funny! I used this exercise for **brainstorming purposes,** and it gave me different ideas for angles and for positioning items for a current project that I'm working on."

Tjerja Geerts, Amstelveen, The Netherlands

No Rules!

Most of us have a favorite sport, something we enjoy playing or enjoy watching. As familiar as we are with the *various rules* **and playing environments of our sport,** there is always something we would change to make the sport better in our minds. **Here's your chance. Take out a piece of paper and write down five things you would change about your favorite sport. It can be a change in the rules or in the playing environment.** The trick is to let your mind go from the obvious rule changes to the absurd. Change the playing field or court, monkey with the number of players, remove protective gear—whatever you think would make the game spectacular to watch!

Dude, Nice Koala Pinky!

One of the most unique parts of our anatomy is the fingerprint. It is completely our own, no one has the same. While most fingerprints are roughly the same shape, depending on how they are inked and applied, **interesting shapes can appear.** You're going to play a little with that today. Most offices have a rubber stamp and ink pad. If you can't find an ink pad, take a pencil and rub an area of darkened pencil on a sheet of paper. Run each of the fingertips of one hand through either the ink pad or pencil rubbing and create five different fingerprints on a piece of sketch paper. Now create a different animal out of each fingerprint by sketching around and through it.

Tick, Tick, Tick, Tick, BOOM!

Sounds surround us everyday. Many have become so common to us that we have stopped hearing them altogether. If visual perspective can be obtained by investigating more closely the common visuals we see everyday, then the common sounds we hear everyday should be examined as well. That will be your task today. Using only the capital letters A, B, C and D as graphic elements, create a visual for the following sounds:

Airplane flying overhead
Dog barking
Sandwich wrapper crinkling
Stomach growling
People typing

inspired by Richard Wilde

What's a "Dot-Com?"

Assemble a design capsule. Collect things from today that you find inspiring. Perhaps a CD cover, a font, a *HOW* magazine, a photograph, a board game, a cooking recipe. Anything you want. Put it in a safe place to open ten years from today.

I Knew He'd Have a Book of Potions, Right?

We are a society of lists. We make lists for everything from groceries to daily chores. There is comfort and security in lists. There are also ideas buried at the bottom of lists, ideas that we never would have found if we didn't make the list. We can all improve our ability to make lists. Your task is to make a list, not of produce or rooms to vacuum, but something far more sinister. Make a list of at least thirty items of things you would find in a mad scientist's lab.

HE'S ALLLIIIIIVVVE!

Sharpie; Shirt Pocket; Laundry Bill

If the old saying is true, "every picture tells a story," then three pictures should tell the story even better. Your task today is to tell a story in three photographs. Grab a digital camera. The idea is to take three consecutive pictures that tell a story. The pattern is "object," "action" and "effect." For instance, if your first photo was your empty chair at work, and your second photo was your boss in your office looking at his watch, the third photograph might be your personal items boxed up on your desk. Create three separate photo-stories using this method. Just make sure you're on time when you start!

BEVERLY HILLS

Is That a Diamond-Studded Coffee Mug?

Each one of us has dreamt, at some point in our lives, what it would be like to be rich and famous, living in Beverly Hills, shopping on Rodeo Drive, walking an overtly pink poodle with more bling around her neck than the NBA bench-warmer down the street. We've imagined, if even for a moment, what that life of *luxury* is really like. Oh, the crazy things we would own! Let's imagine it one more time, if even for just this exercise. Your task is to write down ten things a single woman living in Beverly Hills would own.

"As I began to make my list, ***I found that I was thinking like a man.*** So, I tried to think like a woman. For example, one of my first thoughts was that a rich, single woman in Beverly Hills would own an exotic sports car. Then I realized that a Ferrari would be a Top 10 item on MY list, not necessarily a woman's. Though there may be some women who would purchase an exotic sports car, they might be few in comparison to women who desire a shoe collection the size of Imelda Marcos'. I asked myself if material wealth can be expressed in feminine or masculine ways. A "sports car" seemed masculine until I expanded the concept to "a pink sports car to match a pink handbag."

This exercise taught me that even a "bad" idea can become a "good" idea with the right twist.

I also learned how little I know about how women think."

John Kleinpeter, Irvine, CA

Hold On, I'm Folding My Quarter

Money is so 20th century. Credit cards are used for almost everything these days. It seems that traditional bills and coins are going the way of the dodo as we move closer and closer to a cashless society. It's your task to save the helpless bartering system through the power of design! It's your task to redesign money. But don't just redesign what the bills and coins look like. Think about how they are used, and what the alternatives might be. Are they bills and coins at all? Do bills need another shape? What materials are they made from? Consider all aspects of the concept of barter, both in the practicality of the objects and the value of the individual items.

Take a Seat

The park bench really is an under-appreciated ally. When you're tired, it's there. When you need a place to tie your shoe, it's there. When there are pigeons to be fed, it's there. It deserves its just reward. A face-lift! Your task is to come up with a new design or concept for the park bench. Consider what a park bench is used for, what environment it is typically found in and how to defend it against undesirable visitors. You can add to it, subtract from it, whatever you'd like. The only restriction is that it has to maintain its primary purpose…

to be sat on!

What Is That Thing Dangling From Your Other Arm?

In basketball terms, the "off" hand is the player's weak hand, the one they use least. As most people are right-handed, the "off" hand is often the left hand. As most players are right-handed, the left hand is used little, but the player who learns to use the "off" hand can secure an advantage. We're going to use our "off" hand a little right now. Using whichever hand is your "off" hand, create a squiggle on a piece of paper. Nothing too intricate, just a very simple squiggle. Now use your "strong" hand to create something sports-related out of that squiggle. It could become a piece of equipment, a player or a scene, whatever you might see.

Three Things

Look around your area and find three objects that would fit on a standard piece of paper. Take these three objects over to your photocopier or scanner. Arrange the items so that they overlap, but do not extend past the edges of the resulting copy. Once you have these three objects copied onto a piece of paper, **your task is to find the shape of an animal in the images.** Turn the paper in any direction, fill in negative space, be creative. Use a pencil or pen to draw out the animal on the photocopy.

Linda Lauro-Lazin, New York, NY

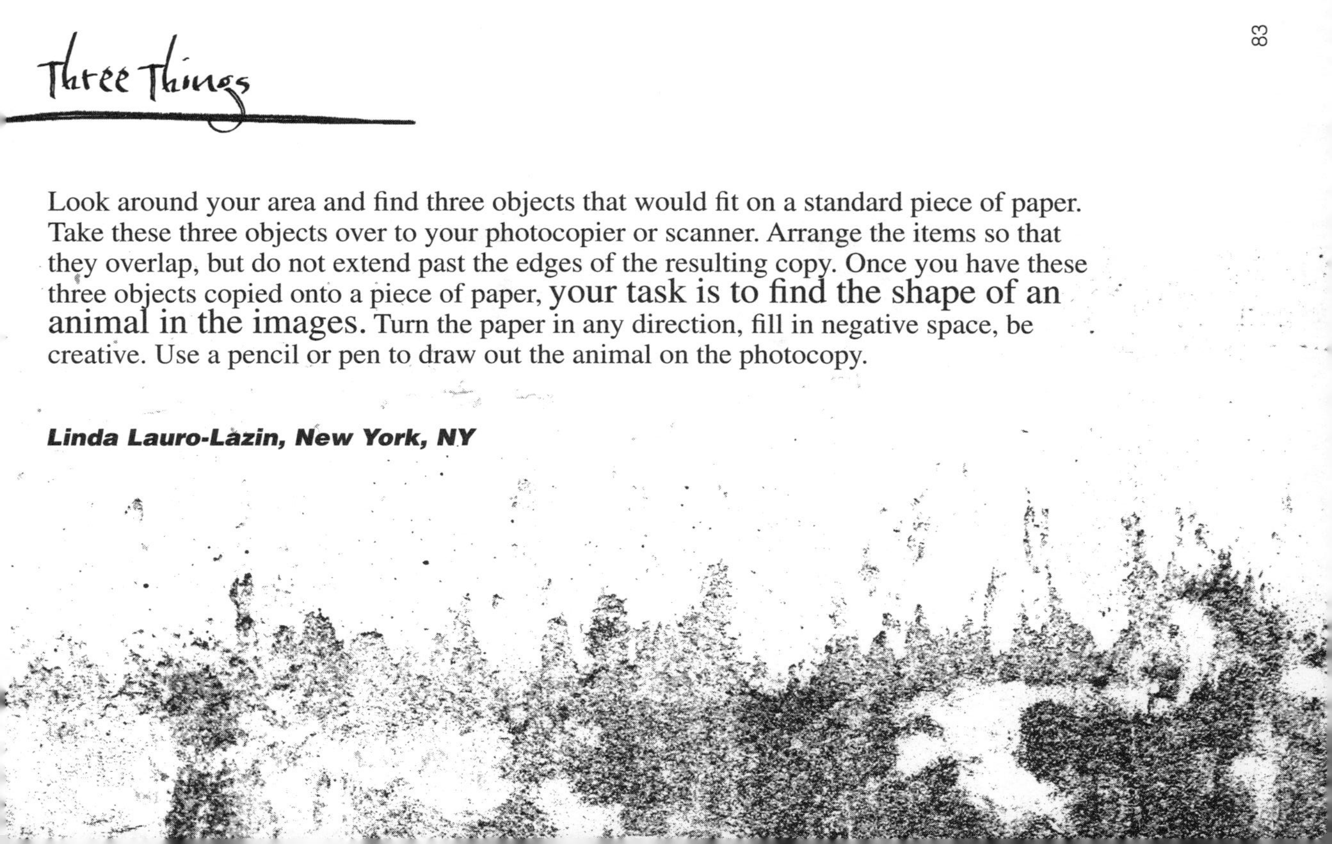

You Got a "D" in Font Selection?

As kids, the day report cards went home was a **frightening** day. How will mom and dad react? What did I get in math? Do I really play well with others? Regardless of the subject, we wanted a good report from our teachers, right? Now that we are all grown up, we no longer have to live in fear of the report card… until now! You'll need one other willing participant for this exercise. Get a friend and create report cards for one another. Subjects can be as straight-forward as "Works well with others," but it'll be more fun if comments are specific to your environment and if you throw a little humor into the mix. You could even work together to create one for the entire studio or team and then grade others. Don't forget to attach that handwritten note from the teacher at the bottom!

Can Anyone Direct Me to the Perfume Aisle?

If there is any one retail outlet more intimidating than the local giant home improvement warehouse hardware mecca, point it out, please. You can get lost just locating a shopping cart. One thing is certain: the target audience of these emporiums is heavily male. Now imagine you are asked to consult on a new brand of über-spacious hardware paradise, this one targeting women. List at least twenty ideas to make the local oversized hardware warehouse appeal to a female demographic.

STCARD

INTERVIEW WITH

Denise Weyrich

The burden on design instructors is much greater than most of us give credit for. Think about the goal of an instructor in any creative industry. They have to not only be proficient and educated in the execution of the medium, they also have to be able to express relevant opinions, provide options without leading students down predefined paths, and give appropriate feedback to a group of people as diverse as they come. In addition, they have the added pressure of possibly being the only connection a student has to the medium, or the subject of the class. The instructor has to communicate the value of the medium in their own life, be caring, have a natural desire to teach, and above all, they have to be passionate. ***That's a lot to lay on one person.*** It's also the choice of thousands of industry professionals and collegiate professors for the very same reason.

Denise Weyhrich is one of these. Accepting the challenge of leading the future of creative thinking in the classroom, Denise had to clearly define her own philosophy on the importance and origins of creativity before she could ever communicate it to a group of students. "Creativity is always a part of life," Denise states. "It is just a matter of how to use it. That simple privilege—to be free to create, to explore and to play—is what propels me out of bed. Creativity and inspiration seem linked, for they are very individual and organic. There is no single solution for either. Creativity looks at the options and both must be open to play and discovery."

Among other responsibilities a design instructor has is the underlying need to not only teach the basic skills to execute in individual mediums, but to encourage and nurture an environment of problem-solving and original thought. *"I loved the MFA world at Syracuse University," Denise begins, "because they taught that radical thinking cannot be ignored. Professor John Sellers taught* research, research and research, *while Richard Wilde taught play, play and play.* In teaching, the trick is to assist the students in understanding how they think through a problem—to know how to solve a problem creatively. The studious, linear, left-brain thinkers need to look around and expand their world of influences, really loosen up and have some fun again. The radical right-brainers need to actually record their ideas, research, expand on their ideas, and recognize the value of their ideas when ideas come so easily for them.

"In the classroom, the goal is to create a safe environment where students could be creative and really design. So often we push to create portfolio pieces, but **a lifestyle of creative thinking is much more important.** Why design if you don't love designing? Designing means creating options and exploring, being creative and not stressing out over it. So we must allow opportunities to be creative, by doing warm-up exercises that parallel the project and allow exploration. Sometimes we need to change the focus from producing products to learning the creative design process over and over again."

As would seem appropriate, most creative-medium instructors are either working creatives or were at one time. One of the challenges in teaching is the flow between teaching and learning. "To inspire and encourage students is the same for a colleague, friend or family member," Denise says. "To inspire and encourage others I have to understand the individual and do the project as well. The 'walk in their shoes' type of experience keeps me in touch. It wears you out, but the payoff is huge. Thinking around the problem and thinking in opposites always works. If the project is about packaging, visit a foreign grocery store where you cannot read a word, but you still understand the products. Walks the aisles and see what is out there in colors, forms, type, illustration. If the project is about type and symbols, try making letters out of 3-D forms, thus exploring a sculptural solution to a 2-D problem. If the project is for kids, question how an old guy would view it, and what about it would really tick him off. Thinking in opposites creates radical thinking and opens up new solutions.

"Keeping an open mind to new discoveries and unique view points are the greatest rewards. The old 'zig when others zag' works. Back in the 1970s, there was a grad student who framed her baby's soiled diapers and exhibited them for her masters' art project. It was creative, but it was also poop! But I still remember it, it made an impact on me.

Sometimes really good poop works."

Finally, hope for all of us!

Denise Weyhrich
Seeds Fine Art Exhibitions
www.seedsfineart.org

What the Heck Is a Quince?

Since we were children, we played association games. Whether it is colors, the alphabet or numbers, we naturally associate certain categories with equivalent descriptions or adjectives. You're going to do a little of this right now. Here are a few items and categories. **Your task is to list on a piece of paper three things that meet the criteria described.** Remember, it doesn't have to be the EXACT item; it can sound like it, be part of the answer, etc:

1) a tv show, personal hygiene product and a vegetable that begin with the letter "R."

2) a musical group, movie title and drink that all have a color in the name.

3) an actor or actress, an animal and a city name that all have a number in their title.

4) An office supply product, a song title and a musical instrument that all have a shape in the name.

5) A food item, an insect and a car model that all have a descriptive word regarding size in their name.

Survival of the Fittest

We all need a little help sometimes. Whether it's stopping for directions or figuring out how to change out the toner cartridge, **even the bravest of men would admit they could use some direction every once in a while** (ya, right!) When put in situations that seem hopeless, most of us would treasure a survival handbook to help get us through. Whether it's a diagram of a particular procedure, or simply a list of substances to avoid, the survival handbook can be a priceless piece of literature. Your task today is to create just such a handbook. For what, you might ask? Choose three situations that could arise in your current environment, from being locked in the bathroom to running out of felt tip pens. Then, on sketch paper or notebook paper, either diagram out or write out the method or ways to get out of the situation. Simple line drawings speak universally, while a description of the action helps immensely as well.

There is ALWAYS a Better Way

This exercise has been around longer than rats. Well, almost. Since man first desired to rid himself of pesky rodents, there have been contraptions and devices created to do in those dastardly critters. Today is no different. In honor of some of the greatest thinkers in history, your challenge today will be to do what they couldn't–create a better mousetrap. Factor in either your putrid disgust or budding fondness for the furry scavengers in designing how to best… umm… dispose of the visitors.

Why Can't I Have an Evil Lair, Too?

We've seen the imagery dozens of times. The mad scientist's evil laboratory. The question we should be asking isn't, "What are his evil plans?" but rather, "What IS he making with all those beakers and Bunsen burners in the background?" Regardless of the evil concoction brewing behind him, it's time we made our own evil concoction with beakers and tubes. **On a piece of sketch paper, grab a pencil and sketch out your very own evil laboratory glass beaker/tube/Bunsen burner trail around the page.** Start in the upper left corner, and create a labyrinth of beakers and tubes, creating paths for the liquid or gas to travel. Throw in your own transport vehicles to get the elixir from one place to another, but remember, it always ends up in a steaming beaker at the end, to be consumed by the doctor himself!

If You Cross Your Eyes Like That, They'll Stay That Way

If we all learned to laugh at ourselves more, the world would be a better place.

And you can't laugh at yourself until you do something funny, so today you're going to do that. Grab a digital camera. Take ten photos of yourself making ten different funny faces. Now laugh. **It's funny!**

You Want an ACME WHAT?

Like Wile E. Coyote in the Road Runner cartoons of old, ***create a trap*** to catch the speedy bird. It can be constructed of natural objects (cactus, boulders, etc.), or something mechanically sophisticated that would have been ordered from Acme. Once your trap is set, outline all the things that could go wrong so that in the end, the Road Runner gets away and Coyote is wrapped in bandages.

Kevin Ehlinger, Avon, MN

i tried it

"If one of the primary methods of maintaining creative fire is to ***revert to a child-like perspective*** and see the world through a child's eyes, what better way than to evoke such great childhood memories? Who didn't love that cartoon? For me, it was always 'Why is everything the Coyote tries based on some strange fascination with split-second timing?' I always thought that the Coyote should stop wasting time on trying to trap him while he was running and stick to the ideas that got the Road Runner to stop first. Coyote always did this with food, but doesn't the Road Runner have to sleep at some point? **What happened to good old-fashioned stalking at night?** I would wait until the Road Runner is asleep, and use my Acme-purchased, remotely flown model stealth plane to fly overhead and stun the Road Runner with heat-seeking stun darts, and then I could simply walk into his camp and bag him at my leisure.

That is, unless the heat-seeking stun darts change course because Coyote is hotter than the Road Runner, and Coyote is targeted instead.

But what're the odds of that?"

Derek Johnson
Milwaukee, WI

Where Was This 25 Years Ago?

Look outside your window. Right now. OK, cubicle dwellers... go FIND a window! Now look around for the nearest large tree. Not a sapling or young tree, but a hearty tree with big limbs. If you don't see one, imagine one from your neighborhood or even your childhood. Got the image of the tree? Good. You've been waiting to do this all your life. **You're going to design the perfect treehouse for that tree.** Don't just think of what YOU could build, or what is "normal" to have, think of the FANTASTIC features that any kid (or adult) would dream about.

Defend Yourself!

As any sane person will tell you, ***there will be a time when the area we currently live in will be overrun by hordes of flesh-craving zombies.*** Naturally, we have all prepared for this inevitability, correct? Of course we have. The task today, in case this vital piece of preparation has eluded your usually comprehensive safety regimen, is to devise your zombie survival plan. Take into consideration the physical desires and limitations of the zombie onslaught, and create not only defense mechanisms (like where the safest place would be to go and how you would get there), but also attack plans. What would you use as weapons? Where could you go to escape the mob? How would you get information about infected areas? You're leaving this guide for those who follow you, so leave the best plan you can in case you yourself become one of the walking dead!

Agency Oz

Laws are here for our protection. They bring order in an otherwise chaotic environment. Most laws are based on written, definable foundations, but some are what sports folks refer to as "unwritten" laws. "Unwritten" laws aren't true laws—but you still should obey them. For instance, in baseball, if you're winning by fifteen runs in the top of the ninth inning, you don't steal a base. It's not against the rules, but it's showing up the other team, and thus qualifies as something you probably shouldn't do. In our creative lives, we rarely run across any formal laws, written or unwritten, but what if we had to create a set of laws for our work environment? That's your task today. Create a set of laws that are strictly internal and reflect the current conditions for your place of employment. These laws should pertain solely to the creative aspect of the business and should be unique to your situation. They can deal with design choices like color or fonts, people on your team, or dealing with clients. They're not intended to be restrictive, just fun. And no one should end up in the slammer!

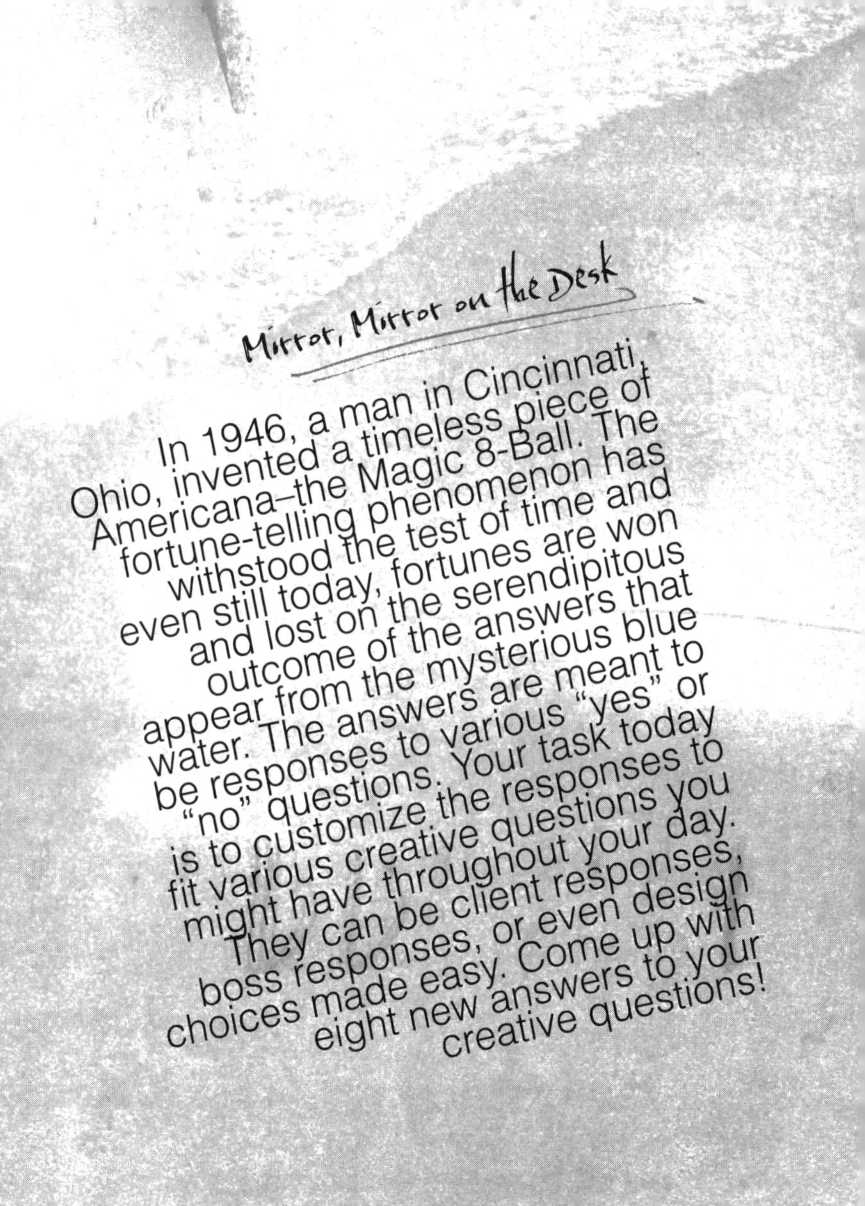

Mirror, Mirror on the Desk

In 1946, a man in Cincinnati, Ohio, invented a timeless piece of Americana–the Magic 8-Ball. The fortune-telling phenomenon has withstood the test of time and even still today, fortunes are won and lost on the serendipitous outcome of the answers that appear from the mysterious blue water. The answers are meant to be responses to various "yes" or "no" questions. Your task today is to customize the responses to fit various creative questions you might have throughout your day. They can be client responses, boss responses, or even design choices made easy. Come up with eight new answers to your creative questions!

Can You Feel the Love?

In 1784, a man by the name of Valentin Haüy pressed a coin into the hand of a blind boy outside his church. The boy, feeling the generous gift might have been a mistake, called out the denomination by the feel of the coin. Haüy had an epiphany. He could teach the blind to read based on touch. Haüy used an alphabet based on Roman letters and began a school for the blind. A boy named Louis Braille attended the school, and had the idea to use a series of dots, which he felt would be more easily discernable by touch—and so braille was born. While braille uses a series of dots and dashes to communicate letter forms, our task today is to consider other forms of touch-sensitive communication. If braille didn't exist, what alternative forms of touch-sensitive communication could you devise for the following items:

water
movie
danger
president
cat

Remember, it has to be based on touch, so no sounds, smells or tastes involved! Consider how the blind could distinguish these items if they opened a book and these words appeared.

Excuse Me, Your Three o' Clock Is Here

47 floors of office workers, hundreds and hundreds of people. You enter the building and you're immediately greeted by the liaison between you down here and them up there... the receptionist. The receptionist's job is to communicate to someone up there that you down here require their attention. The usual choice of communication is the telephone or intercom. But today is National Give The Receptionist The Boot Day. Today, you're in charge of coming up with a better system to let them up there know you're down here. Either by writing out the idea or sketching it on paper, develop a better solution to alert someone within the company that they have a visitor or that there is some attention needed at the front desk.

That Looks Just Like Nothing!

Our lives are filled with pattern. We see patterns in textiles, building materials, nature, even food. With as much pattern as we see, it begs the question, "Is anything random anymore?" Time to explore the answer. Grab a digital camera. Your task today is to take ten pictures of things in your environment that have no pattern or order. Find things that are completely random. Go!

"With my more conceptual imagery, it is always a question of how to get outside the box to gather ideas. This exercise got me out of the box in a hurry. I started envisioning where I might find complete randomness in the middle of Los Angeles! I thought possibly a group of trees that were not purposefully planted, or maybe an accident where something was smashed, dropped or spilled. Then I thought how cool it would be if, within a project, I conceded even those things one would expect to be random to this overwhelming patterning we live in. My mind started reeling with images of spilled food in the kitchen splattering into discernable images or even messages spelled out! Or a handful of coins dropped bouncing into neat piles of pennies, nickels and dimes! Until the right client comes around, I think I just found my next personal project!"

James Maciariello, Los Angeles, CA

I TRIED IT

Nice Hood Ornament!

There are throngs of people out there whose only job is to improve our cars. From GPS satellite navigation systems to windshield wipers that sense rain, automobile improvements are coming faster and stronger than ever before. Today, you join these honorable pioneers. Your task today is to create three improvements to the modern car. They can be mechanical, cosmetic, futuristic, sensible, small, large, whatever. They don't even have to be obtainable or even possible—their only restriction is that they have to make the modern car better in some way.

Holy Nightmares, Batman!

The Boy Wonder could have used this exercise. If you do any creative writing at all, a thesaurus is a trusted friend. ***The thesaurus is the creative writer's Pantone book.*** But there are also times in our creative lives that we wish we could provide people with a thesaurus to help them use the right word, in reaction to our work. There have been numerous times that we have sat down with a client to show them the comps, and their reaction wasn't exactly what we hoped for, nor did it tell us what they really thought of the direction we chose. If they had, say, a Reaction Thesaurus, it might help. A book they could thumb through and find the right word that means exactly what you think it means, because you wrote it! That's your task today. Create a Reaction Thesaurus for your clients to use when reacting to your work. Include the good with the bad, but in each instance, include what the meaning is, so that everyone is clear when you show the comps, and they say, **"That's Nice, I Like It,"** everyone knows what happens next! Start with ten entries and see if that is enough to cover the gamut. If you're feeling saucy, create a little book and give it to your clients. They could use the help!

white or wheat?

Mmmmm… sandwich! Is there anything better for lunch than a good, old-fashioned sandwich? OK, maybe you have an item or two you would prefer, but there's no question the sandwich is the quintessential portable noontime meal. Everyone has their favorite sandwich. Are you thinking of it right now? Good. Now imagine that you didn't have ANY of the ingredients you're picturing right now. You could probably get by with something else. Well, think again. Your task today is to create the world's worst sandwich, but not out of the ingredients you're used to using. You're going to replace them, but with items that might seem, shall we say, less satisfying. Create a sandwich with these ingredients:

BREAD: Choose anything you'd find in a gym locker

CONDIMENTS: Choose anything in paste form

CHEESE: Choose anything that would melt over a fire

VEGETABLES: Choose anything found in a hardware store

MEATS: Choose anything with a smooth texture

Prehistoric Voicemail?

One of the most influential pieces of technology to enter our lives in the last twenty years is the cell phone. It has made anyone reachable at virtually any time. It has changed the way we communicate. Those who grew up pre-cell phone often lament about a time when a car accident in the middle of nowhere meant hiking for hours. How did people get by?! That's your task today, to imagine exactly that. Theorize with either words or sketches what the mobile communication device would have been for the following eras:

Medieval Europe
Biblical Times
The Old West
The 1970s

Consider the trends of the day, what resources the people had at their disposal, distance restrictions, etc. How did people in each of these eras communicate in a mobile way, the way we do with cell phones?

Et Tu, Rombus 3000?

Robots have saturated science fiction for over a century. While many robotic advancements have been made in society, the seemingly endless promise of the household robot still is just a promise. ***But what if we could help that promise become a reality by defining exactly the type of robot we would want? That is your challenge today.*** Describe in words or sketch on a sheet of paper what powers and abilities your perfect household robot would have. Don't limit yourself to just what's doable today. Think about all the applications, feasible or not, that your robot could perform for you. Or with you. Or to you. Oh… ummm… huh… wait, were you saying something?

Para-Military... Pens?

You're going to get a little competitive on this one. Grab a few willing souls for a little base-jumping expedition. You're going to engage in a little friendly target practice. Each of you should get your garden variety ball point pen, cap firmly in place. You're going to drop those pens from at least a second-story drop towards a predefined target area. First, define the target area by taping a square on the ground. Next, each of you needs to devise a way to drop your pen into the area... with a makeshift parachute. Use whatever parachute materials you think will do the job. But there's a catch. You need to rig your pen so that it is standing up when it lands. How, you may ask? You might create some sort of base for the pen that allows it to land standing straight up, whether that's two other pens taped to the bottom of the para-pen, a drink coaster; whatever you think will allow the pen to land standing straight up. Whoever can get their pen closest to the target while remaining straight up and down, wins.

BOMBS AWAY!

Did You Get That License?

License plates identify many things about a particular vehicle, none less graphic than the home state of the registration. Each state offers multiple license plate designs to choose from, some celebrating historic events, some celebrating attractive qualities about the state. What a license plate doesn't give is any insight to the owner of the vehicle, outside of the occasional vanity plate. Your challenge today is to rethink the license plate by moving away from state-centered branding and into occupational or hobby-related branding. You are going to create three license plate designs for the following three owners:

Hip-hop music artist

CIRCUS CLOWN

Motivational Speaker

Consider both the requirements of a license plate (numbers/letters, tags, etc.) and how the plate would appear on the vehicle. Let's roll!

I'll Take a Double Scoop of Pay-Toilet Please

EEEEwwwwwwwwwww!

That's your desired reaction to this exercise. Simply put, come up with the **nastiest flavored ice cream** that you can imagine. Not only that, consider what you would serve it with. What would the cone and the toppings be made out of to complement your filthy flavor? **Ooohhhh.** (burp)

Can You Get Curds at the Deli Down the Street?

Nursery rhymes are a part of just about every toddler's learning environment. The interpretation of common experiences is a part of just about every creative's learning environment. Now, the two shall meet! Your task today is to illustrate the fan favorite "Little Miss Muffet" nursery rhyme using only the following graphical elements:

The letter A
The letter M
A square
A straight line
A circle

You can use the graphical elements as many times as you like to illustrate the story, but you must do it in four frames, and they must be completely black and white, no gradients or other colors. The letterforms cannot be broken apart; they must stay intact, but all elements can be resized to your heart's content.

Little Miss Muffet
Sat on a tuffet
Eating her curds and whey;
Along came a spider,
Who sat down beside her
And frightened Miss Muffet away.

(inspired by Richard Wilde)

Our Janitor Doesn't Look Like That!

There are signs posted around every office in the world, signs that warn us of impending danger, bathroom segregation or even which way the exit is. These signs become such a sterile bummer. What if those signs were changed to an international pictorial language that not only identified the door, room, fire extinguisher, etc. but added art to the space? Forget the shapeless figures and celebrate the difference between men and women, janitors and upper management! Create new signs for:

- Men's/Women's room
- Fire Extinguisher
- Janitor's Closet
- Executive Washroom
- Parking Garage
- Exit

Denise Weyhrich, Orange, CA

And the Pitch... TOUCHDOWN!

Sports are a way of life. Many of us grew up around at least one sport, and most likely, we were and are engaged in multiple sporting activities. We root for our favorite sports teams, play in sports leagues and idolize sports heroes. With so many sports and so little time to either watch or engage in them, something has to be done to satisfy our thirst for more sports. That's where you come in. Your task for today, in the name of consolidating our sports intake, is to combine two sports into one. Create the scenarios, the rules, the things that are taken from one sport and transfered to the other. Consider the playing environment, the ball (if there is one!), the players, the equipment and the rules.

Pimp My Catapult!

There have been some ingenious vehicles in history. Like, ancient history. Since the wheel was invented, clever inventors have used it to transport everything from people to war machines. These vehicles were rarely luxurious, mind you, with the exception of the occasional royal transport. Your task today is to make them so. Choose one of the following historical transports to "soup up" with all the modern upgrades you can imagine:

Roman Chariot
Medieval Catapult
Old West Stage Coach
European Carriage
Oriental Rickshaw

Deck the vehicle out in all the modern luxuries we have grown to desire. The only restriction is that it can't lose its original purpose: to get from point A to point B. Spinners optional.

INTERVIEW WITH
BRIAN SACK

We've heard stories like this many times. **A creative works for years in an industry, creating quality work but getting little recognition for it.** Then, the strangest of things finds some light, grows out of control, and all of a sudden, they're known as **"Hot Pants"** in the creative industry. *They've finally got the recognition they deserve, there's a certain buzz around them, but it's for the oddest of projects.*

Meet Brian Sack. Brian has been writing for Madison Avenue shops for years. He decides agency life isn't for him, goes out on his own chasing down fame and fortune as a writer and entertainer, and falls into semi-stardom online with, of all things, an eBay auction. Brian sold a pair of leather pants, circa 1985, and his description for the auction brought a more-than-adequate selling price. His choice to be creative with even the most average of tasks has proven to be fruitful.

MORE →

"I've spent a lot of energy making things less mundane for the benefit of myself and others," Sack starts. "Having been cursed with the entertainer gene, I've always approached everything from the standpoint of how I might be able to make it enjoyable—which to me means making it funny. I've done that with pretty much everything I've had to write, whether it be an e-mail or an attempt to get out of a parking ticket. *Overall, I've wasted countless hours of my life trying to liven things up for no other reason than I'm afraid of being considered boring."*

A lesson to all creatives that professionalism is in the details, Brian's character is a testament to living the creative life. Brian's definition of creativity is simple. "Creativity means producing something original which has value to others because it makes them laugh, cry or think." That might tend to put a lot of pressure on someone to constantly produce creative work, but Brian doesn't see it that way. He finds the pressure he feels to produce creative work is relieved through discipline and routine. **"The best thing I ever did as a writer was discipline myself to not only carry a notebook and pen everywhere," Brian says, "but to use them the moment something occurred to me.** I never realized how many ideas disappear into the ether within seconds—no matter how much you tell yourself you'll remember them later.

When I'm having a hard time creatively, I gather all the notebooks and transfer the ideas into a bigger notebook which stays on my desk at home. A great deal of the time, seeing these little germs of ideas I've written down over the weeks is all it takes to spark something. Looking in my notebook right now I see 'Stalin's goal buddy.' I have no idea what that means, but I believed it to be funny at the time. *Maybe it'll be something some day."*

Like any creative medium, writing comes with the same creative struggles to do the one thing we all need to do to create great work—start. Brian's motivation to create is the same for any medium. "What gets me writing is actually writing," Brian shares. "My biggest obstacle is distraction, lack of focus. I need the structure a routine provides, so **I get up at six every morning** and try and keep to a schedule that makes me productive. Sometimes it works, and sometimes it doesn't and I lose focus and wind up all over the place. I find having a solid deadline is a good motivation to get something done, so I've gotten in the habit of asking folks to pin me down to a particular date and time, lest I drag something out for all eternity."

Like any of us have done that.

Brian Sack,
Banterist
www.banterist.com

I Think It Needs More (Insert Noun Here)

In 1953, a man by the name of Leonard Stern invented the classic party game, Mad Libs. By creating stories minus some descriptive parts and leaving those to the uninformed audience, grammar component by grammar component, Leonard created a fun way to learn that context is everything. Today, you're going to fill in a Mad Lib by supplying a few parts right now, then you're going to create your own. On a piece of paper, write down your answers to the following sentence components:

1. adjective
2. position in a creative firm
3. adjective
4. noun
5. adjective
6. noun
7. verb
8. market or target audience
9. noun
10. authority figures
11. adjective

Now drop those sentence pieces into the following story:

"It sounded like a (1. adjective) idea at the time. The client obviously disagreed. Our (2. position in a creative firm) warned us against using THAT (3. adjective) of a (4. noun) in the ad. He felt that people would have an (5. adjective) reaction to the way the (6. noun) was (7. verb)ing. We thought it was funny. We thought the (8. market or target audience) market could laugh at itself. We were wrong. The only one laughing was the (9. noun) that came into the pitch after us. We could hear them laughing as we left. When we got back, our (10. authority figures) awaited us. Sometimes the design industry can be straight up (11. adjective)."

Now that you have the hang of it, create your own Mad Lib about your environment or an experience that is unique to you. Start by writing a story, then go back and remove some of the key descriptors and subjects and replace them with sentence component placeholders. Have someone you know give you the components and read the story out loud.

Fore! Five! Watch Out!

In 1867, the Ladies' Putting Club in St. Andrews, Scotland opened, marking the beginning of the wonderment that is miniature golf. Miniature golf has entertained countless millions with putting holes so complex and fantastic, even the avid linksman could find joy in a three-putt. From windmills to alligator mouths, miniature golf holes are an architectural phenomenon. Well, maybe not THAT divine, but still. Your task today is to create your very own miniature golf hole, complete with whatever obstacle you want to design. Make use of space and depth, use physics to move the ball around and don't forget the purpose… to drive otherwise sane people bonkers. If you're feeling spicy, create another hole, and so on, finishing with a complete 18. And some form of brain damage.

Fore!

Is That a Fire Pole?

Creative-minded architects have raised the bar on luxurious modern home design, from including escalators to rotating fireplaces to poolside waterfall wet bars. The imagery and opulence can be fantastic. You might not want a home with every imaginable feature (OK, we would too) but you're going to get a chance to at least create one. ***Your challenge today is to create the one fantastic feature you'd build into your next home if money was no object and anything could be done.*** And don't stop there. List all the remarkable advancements your dream home would have. Just be sure to stock the wet bar.

I'm New and Improved!

Ad guys spend all day and all night creating ads for various products and services, including headlines and body copy, graphics and visuals. Photo shoots and illustrations are involved. Someone even chooses the right font. Sometimes.

Regardless of the product or service, creating an ad for someone else is easy compared to something a little more personal... say, you! Your task today is to create an ad for you. That's right, you. You're the product. Or service. Whichever fits best. Come up with the headline, the body copy, the visual, the whole thing. Even the font choice. Sell you like you've never been sold before. That didn't come out right...

Did He Just Tell Me to Steal Third or is His Nose Running?

Signs have been a part of professional baseball since 1869. Coaches and players use signs to communicate plays and relay instructions to runners and batters who are too far away to be told discreetly. Signs typically involve a series of movements by the coaches, ***like touching their nose,*** then the brim of their hat, then wiping their arm, then clapping. Each movement means something, and in the proper order, communicates the play to the player. Wouldn't it be nice if we could develop a similar system to communicate in situations where we don't want anyone to know what we're saying? Like client meetings, when the person presenting has toilet paper stuck to his shoe. Sure would be nice to alert him of that without yelling it across the room. That's your task today. You are going to develop a series of signals and signs to communicate key messages to one another. The messages can be anything from "Don't quote a price!" to "The job will take six weeks." Make up what messages need to be communicated as well as the signs involved. Now get up there and bunt home a run.

How Do You Say "Red" In Caveman?

Quick, think of the color blue! How about yellow? It's not that hard, is it? Now try this… **think of the color delphinium.** Not so much? How about **celadon?** Blank, huh? It seems we are conditioned to picture only the colors we can define. Makes sense. We can provide an educated guess to a shade if given a name that carries certain characteristics, like lettuce or garden (both shades of green, of course.) With this in mind, your task today is to rename the eight colors most commonly found in a box of crayons. The twist is that you will be renaming them with certain categories of people as your target. For instance, if the category is "florists," your name for the color green might be "stem," red might be "rose," and so on. The colors in an eight-pack of crayons typically are: blue, red, yellow, green, purple, orange, black and brown. Here are your categories:

Dog Catchers
Knights of the Round Table
Soft-Drink Lovers
High School Students
Baseball Fans

Choose one of these groups and rename the colors to appeal to the specific group. If you're feeling colorful, move on to the box of sixty-four crayons!

So Should I Stop Where I Am or Run?

Cross any major intersection on foot and you'll most likely run into the safety valve of street-crossing: the walk/don't walk sign. The walk/don't walk sign tells us when it's safe to cross the street when we see the graphic of the person walking. When that person walking turns to a defiant hand symbol, we know we need to wait until the next light. These symbols also use color to communicate (white for 'walk' and red for 'stop.') Your task today is to take the same concept and apply it to five situational decisions you make thoughout your day. Think of five polar decisions (decisions that are "one-or-the-other" decisions) you have to make every day, then create the "walk/don't walk" symbol for each decision. The symbol should be simple, as if it's going to be presented on a street corner.

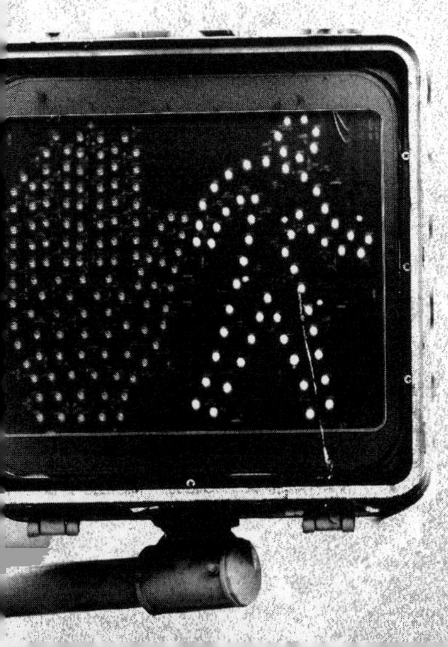

Mmmmmm… Cardboard

Universally, all babies and most young toddlers seem to gravitate toward the packaging and wrapping of a Christmas toy rather than the toy itself. We could just wrap a cardboard box and they'd be just as enthralled. To them, the box IS the toy. Thus, the lesson. Your challenge today will be to create a baby or young toddler's toy where the package is part of the toy. Consider how it would be packaged for the store shelf and how that package would be used in conjunction with the toy to create something that even the most fickle of package-loving children would interact with. Sketch a prototype or write a summary of the concept.

It's Even Got Flaps!

The cardboard box gets squat when ad award season comes around. Who makes an ad for a box anyway? Today, that's going to change. Think about it. If you can market something as rudimentary and utilitarian as a 6" x 6 " x 6" cardboard box, you can market anything, right? Right. So that's your task for today. Come up with an ad for the cardboard box. Create a headline, the body copy, and the visual. Consider primary and secondary uses, construction highlights and customizable options. It can be open or closed, come assembled or flat. And think of the money you'd save on shipping!

Don't Push That Button!

James Bond gets all the cool toys. "Q" gives him everything from X-Ray glasses to belt-buckle weaponry. Why can't the average joe get toys like that? For free? Just because? Here's your chance to, at the very least, put in your request to the IT department.

Your challenge today is to **create the perfect client meeting spy gadgets.** Consider the things that you would need most and what devices could house them for you. Just stay clear of the explosives.

An "E" Ticket Ride

Face it: Adults like amusement park rides, too. Actually, they love them as much as kids do. Something about the **thrill** of a roller coaster or the enchantment of a ride themed after childhood's favorite stories. ***Your task today is to create just such a ride. You're going to create a theme park ride wrapped around your favorite fast-food chain. Now that's a theme! Consider the food items, the store design, graphic elements that are used and marketing themes. Create a ride that proudly expresses that fast-food joint's true value.*** Hold the mayo, please.

"It was 2:30 and I just finished a grueling deadline and had not eaten lunch yet, so I headed to a coffee shop to unwind a bit before tackling the next project. A perfect way to unwind was to write a stream-of-consciousness story with a happy ending. ***When I finished, I felt such relief at just writing nonstop without letting the editor in me scrutinize an idea, or stop one from forming completely.*** I felt lighter, freer and actually had some good stuff in my writing. I am planning to use this exercise in coming up with my 'wish list' of all of the ideas and avenues I'd like to propose for promoting our company's products–no censorship and hopefully a happy ending."

Julia Scannel,
Napa, CA

I Tried It

In a Land Far, Far Away...

Writing a story typically means developing characters, forming a plot, and finding a conclusion. These ingredients to the story-telling soup often take careful planning. But what if you weren't given enough time nor had any idea what to write about? That's exactly what we are going to do. Get a piece of lined paper. On the first line write "Once upon a time..." Now just go. Create characters and storylines based on what is happening around you right now. Don't plan, just start writing, filling in plot issues and character holes as you go. It doesn't have to make total sense, just keep writing until you've filled the paper. At the end, find a one-sentence conclusion, and finish with "and they lived happily ever after."

Can Someone Show Me the Door?

When we enter a building, one thing is for certain: at some point, we're going to want to come back out again. Introducing our best friend at this dire time… the exit sign. The exit sign tells us where the "out" is. It's extremely fortunate that the word "exit" exists in our day and age, or we'd have no idea how to get back out. Or would we? Your task today is to develop an alternative to the exit sign. Without using the word "exit," create a sign that alerts people that this is the way out.

My Totem is Teetering

Monumental carvings, otherwise known as totem poles, moved from houseposts to funerary containers to memorial markers. Since they were traditionally made of wood, most have deteriorated over time, so dating the ceremonial monuments is difficult. We're not going to worry about dating them; we're going to concern ourselves with making our own. Your task is to create your own totem pole. While historically, totem poles evolved to represent social status, yours is going to tell the story of your typical day or week. On a sheet of sketch paper, create a design for your own daily or weekly emotional totem pole.

I'll Take the Double Raptor Meal Deal, Please

Buried deep within that kid's meal deal is the magic convincer. The single greatest toy ever played with… for four minutes. Inexpensive kid's meal deal toys have been a fast food staple forever. From character figures to bathtub buddies, meal deal toys draw kids to extort hard earned cash from unsuspecting parents. How did kids live without them in the past? It's almost incomprehensible. Until now. Your task today is to create the kid's meal deal toy equivalent for these historical child lunch-seekers:

Medieval Times
Biblical Times
Prehistoric Times
The Year 3000
The Old West

List the appropriate "meal deals" for each era, along with THE toy that these kids would sell their sisters to get.

I Didn't Think She Could Eat All of That

Sometimes, pictures don't tell us enough of the story, we need the caption. The description below the photo clues us in to the meaning of the image, or maybe gives an insight to a conversation occurring above. Either way, without the caption, some images are useless, while captions alone don't communicate the whole story; they need accompanying visuals. Go to www.wakeupmybrain.com/cftcm/exercises/photocaptions.pdf. Print the photos that appear in the PDF. Look at each of the photos individually. Your task today is to create five captions for each photo describing what you think is going on in these photos. It can be conversation between characters, it can be a summary of the action, or it can simply be a title to the photo. Here's a hint: the funnier, the better!

I Can't Find the Surprise!

Kids have been going elbow-deep in their cereal boxes for decades. The elusive cereal box toy has delighted breakfast-minded children into firing open box after box looking for the secret prize described on the back. Everything from baseball cards to spy kits have been buried like treasure in the sugary depths of cereal boxes. These toys are typically not targeted to any specific group of children, outside of the occasional gender demographic, but that's all going to change today. Your challenge today is to define the perfect cereal box toy for these "children." You need to imagine as children:

The President of the United States
A Hollywood Stuntman
A Construction Worker
A Magician
A Fry Cook
A Hair Stylist
A Race Car Driver
An Emergency Room Nurse

Sorry, Charlie

Kids love talking animals. Can you blame them? Animators have been piquing the interest of children and adults alike by personifying animals with human traits and characteristics, from the ability to speak and read to whole environments that are made to feel like their human counterparts. What if… animals could really speak and read? What if fish, for instance, could actually understand our language and visual communication? That's your task today. Imagine fish can comprehend visual and verbal communication; they can read and understand. Now imagine you are a surfboard manufacturer. What would you design for the bottom of your surfboards? Whatever sea life is under those surfboards while they are in the water can comprehend the message you put on the bottom. What is it you would say to them? Create the bottom of your surfboard.

We've Got Spirit, Yes We Do!

Ah, the cheerleader. Who doesn't love a cheerleader? Put your hands down. **Cheerleaders rock.** You want to be one. Yes, you do. Stop arguing; yes, you do. Regardless of you living in denial, your task today is to get in touch with your inner cheerleader and create a cheer. Yes, seriously. And it better be a good one, too! Or we'll make you be on the bottom of the human pyramid next time. It seems cheers fall under two categories: 1) Build your team up; 2) Put their team down. We like number two. But that's your call. Create a cheer of at least four lines that either builds your team up or puts down some other team. Teams can be your co-workers, another design firm, a client, your boss, whomever deserves a good cheer. ***Give me an "Exclamation Point!"***

I Wear My Sun-Survivor-Goggle-Glasses at Night

Sunglasses have become essential pieces of any trip out into the daylight. From designer eyewear to cheap grocery store plastics, sunglasses are vital to all glare-challenged surface dwellers. The problem with sunglasses is that they're so one-dimensional. All they do is keep sunlight out of your eyes. Nothing else. Until now. Your challenge today is to create the perfect pair of sunglasses. Think "Eyewear meets Swiss Army Knife." Create a pair of sunglasses that have as many cool, useful gadgets and functions as you can think of. Either draw out this prototype or simply write a narrative. The only restriction is that they still need to keep sunlight out of your eyes!

Mine Has Five Colored Rings!

You're going to design a **logo for the 2016 Olympic Games**. To start designing this new identity, you need to first *assemble category words*–three to six nouns, adverbs, and adjectives–that in general terms best describe the 2016 Olympics. Arrange these three to six words in columns at the top of a piece of paper. Add a seventh word, ***animorphic,*** to these words. Animorphic words are beings or things that, as a concept, exemplify the attributes of the client. We know that NBC doesn't sell peacocks, but because we associate peacocks with being vivid and colorful, we can automatically transfer these attributes to the company. These seven will be the main categories for the project. ***Now it's brainstorming time***. Under each column, write down words that are associated with the heading–no matter how wild or crazy they might seem. Once your page is filled with words under each of the columns, it's time to start the process of forced random connection. Take one word from each column and figure out how to merge them all into one logo. You have to force yourself to make a visual connection between the columns. **In effect, you're force-feeding your head with disparate concepts and then watching for *unexpected connections* to emerge**. You might hit dead ends quickly, but enough visual concepts will bloom to keep you enthusiastic.

Bill Gardner, Wichita, KS

Rest in Peace

Halloween always opens the casket of tombstones and gravemarkings. Written well, tombstones can reveal a great deal about the individual who is buried beneath. Some are poems, some are signature sayings the individual might have used, and some simply are a series of dates and names. Your task today is to create your own tombstone message. The restriction here is it needs to be brief and it need to rhyme. Let the world know what you're about in a few short words.

Box That Ferret, Please

It's all about the packaging these days. Packaging carries the burden of informing us what the contents are, why they're great and what we can use them for. It even tells us if we've seen it on TV. Almost everything comes in some form of prepackaged form. Except things like... pets.

Animals rarely come packaged.

Pet stores might place that new kitten in a carry-home container, but the feline didn't come to the pet store that way. What if they did? Your challenge today is to choose the pet you identify most with, and create the package for that animal if that animal was to come to the store prepackaged. Think about the size of the package, the type of package, the marketing messages on the outside and the needed elements on the inside of the package. And don't forget air holes. You weren't going to forget, were you?

I Already Have That One!

Kids love the happy meal, that marketing-savvy way to combine a junior size burger, fries and fruit punch with some form of inexpensive trinket a child would drool over. **The toy is the key.** A kid could convince his parents to purchase gold plated french fries if it meant getting his hands on that plastic treasure. Adults are far too, well, adult for that. They see right though that charade. Adults would never sell out their precious intake choices for some throw-in gift.

Or would they?

Your task today is to create the adult happy meal toy.

What could you put in a combo meal that would entice an otherwise salad-conscious dietitian to grub on that deep-fat-fried taco? Create a list of your top ten adult happy meal toys.

Interview with
STEVE
MORRIS

www.thinkfeelwork.com. That is the web address of ***Morris! Communications.*** *"Head Honcho" Steve Morris has put together one of the hottest shops in the country, located in the emerging design hotbed of San Diego, CA.* Steve and his team have had the opportunity to work with some amazing clients, churning out ideas that are not only remarkably unique, but intuitively crafted. *How does he manage to cultivate all of these ideas and turn them into reality?* *"You can't develop and nurture ideas without giving them time to live and breathe on their own,"* *Morris says. "You have to take the time to get your head around the problem. First, take the time to identify the problem, and then dive into the creativity element of it. It's not only time, it's also space. When you get into the activity of developing concepts, you need to be in the right mind frame. So often you have to go from production meetings, work, playing with the kids, lunch, to 'Okay, now I have to come up with an idea for this particular ad campaign.' If you're too stressed out, you're likely not ever going to get there, I don't care how much time you have. So, first and foremost, the thing that has to happen is the space. The head space, and then the time to allow it to happen.* ***I actually think that getting out of the environment helps creativity the most.***

You have to have experience to add to what you're doing, and those experiences are the biggest things that fuel creativity. If you exist only in a fishbowl in the design industry, and all that you read are the standard design publications, your ideas will be relatively small. You have to think outside of what you're used to."

So what does creativity mean to Steve Morris? "I think that the definition of creativity is that every human being is very creative, and exercises that creativity. That doesn't mean that they do it for a living, but anyone who is able to see things differently is inherently a creative. That doesn't mean that they're going to use it. And anyone has the ability to problem-solve on any level. It's just to what degree. And if you're openly willing to express it. In kindergarten everyone is an artist. People go back to artwork because they want the cathartic process of expressing themselves. It never went away. It was always there just waiting for them. So I firmly believe that we're all creative, it's just the extent that they accept it within themselves and go about stressing it. It's like working out—the more you do, the better you feel/stronger you're doing to be."

Taking a gander at the studio tells you all you need to know about Steve's philosophy on creativity and his environment. Hardwood floors, bold, professional-grade graffiti on the walls, a wall of windows overlooking Wyatt Earp's saloon across the street.

The design environment definitely plays a role in the creative process.

"When you walk in here," Steve begins, "Hopefully one of the first things that you feel is that this is a creative environment. Secondly, if you were to begin to spend any time with the people that work here, you would understand clearly that this is a creative culture. The core of my nature is a creative and that leads to many different things. It's also my relationship to life and everything around me.

It's not just what I do for a job, but it's who I am as a person, so my environment is so important for me to come into this atmosphere that reflects who I am. So it's not only the space itself, but it's also how we design the space out. How the space sort of works within itself. You know, having grafitti on our walls and what that says not only about our culture but also to our clients and what work we do, what that says about how we think about the environment itself. There are quick gathering spaces. There's always stuff going on. The magnet board, where things are constantly being put up there. It was designed with all of that in mind for it to happen so that it works for our needs."

Steve's relationship to the people he has seen to surround himself with are equally as important.

"Everyone here has a say about their own area. They are playing a role, they should have a say. I want them to put their heart and soul into this, I want them to have a say and some level of control with the outcome. With every employee that is hired here, the second interview happens with everyone in the studio. I want to get a sense of the chemistry, and I want everyone here to have a say about the interviewee who they will be potentially working with." We're tight. We just went rock climbing a few weeks ago together. We watch movies together. There's a pool table, a dart board—they promote playful spontaneity. At any point these guys can drop it, go shoot some darts, get back to work.

That sense of play, of getting out of here as a group, as well as individually... those things are so important."

It doesn't hurt to put up camp in sunny San Diego, either!

Steve Morris
Morris! Communications
www.thinkfeelwork.com

Let's Introduce You to Alex

Alex has had many, MANY jobs. Do you know anyone like that? Anyway, Alex is 39 years old, and has been asked by his landlord (re: mom) to create a list of the various jobs he has had. Unfortunately, his landlord can't read as well as she used to, so Alex, being the tortured artist that he is, decides instead that he will draw his name in the style of each of his previous jobs. Simply by looking at each name, his mom… errr, landlord will be able to understand what job he held. But alas, Alex's hands have fallen off. Happens. He needs you to do it for him. Just draw out Alex's name in a graphic representation that befits his job title. His various jobs were:

1) Cowboy
2) Weightlifter
3) Blacksmith
4) Poolboy
5) Fast Food Fry Cook
6) Gardener
7) Doorman
8) Blackjack dealer

Superman's Not Home Right Now

Is there anything sadder than a pay phone booth these days? With the advent of the cell phone, those once-popular necessities are all but extinct. Try to think of the last time you used a pay phone, and then try to recall the last pay phone you used that was housed in a phone booth. It's been a while, huh? Those phone booths are still around. They didn't get their feelings hurt and leave the country, they just have no purpose in life anymore. It's your job today to give them a purpose. Come up with ten alternative uses for our old friend, the phone booth. They can have the pay phone still housed inside, or you can lose the phone altogether, replace the phone with some other usage, whatever you want. You can even dislodge the phone booth from its home and put it somewhere else. Just don't forget the dimes.

Back In My Day, the Fans Didn't Have Lasers

Sports are a part of our heritage, and have been for centuries. Can you imagine if those first athletes, running foot races in ancient history, could see what sports have become today, with technological advances, athlete enhancements and state-of-the-art facilities? Although our amazement might not be of equal shock value, we're going to put ourselves in their shoes. Your task today is to pick a sport. Any sport. Now, write down what you think that sport will be like in the year 2500 A.D. Consider all the fantastic advances in technology, space travel, science, equipment and players that might be experienced.

How Do I Get Ink Off My Desk Again?

We're too judgmental. Especially with our own work. You hear people say all the time, **"I can't draw."** In actually, they CAN draw, they just don't think it looks like anything, so they stop trying altogether. Maybe that's you. Today, we're going to draw, but we're going to alleviate all the anxiety that the image doesn't look like the object. Right up front, we're going to give you the out: ***IT'S NOT SUPPOSED TO!*** Take out some sketch paper. Now find an object in your area, something small but not coin-sized. Now, you're going to draw this object, but with a catch. You can't look at the paper. Look solely at the object. Don't give in to the urge to look at the paper and see how you're doing, just draw. Look at the paper to see where you want to start, then don't look at it again until you're done. It doesn't have to be one continuous line, you can lift the pencil up, but don't ever look at the paper until you're done. When you're done, you might be surprised at what you see. It won't look much like the image, but you'll definitely be able to see areas that you succeeded in capturing what you saw. And that's a start!

How Do You Draw Music?

Our minds associate images with words. Try it. Close your eyes and think of the word "beauty." You saw pictures, didn't you? Your mind doesn't think abstractly. We put together images with words. Your task today is a little like that. We're going to do an "expressive word." You're going to choose a word, then you're going to draw it out in such a way that it communicates that word in the way you draw it. It doesn't have to be every letter, but the design of the word should express the meaning of the word. For instance, if your word is "music," the *s* might be a treble clef, you might use music notes in the *i*, etc. If your word is "basketball," all the letters might be drawn with the dimples of a basketball as filler. These are just a few examples. Really, it's wide open in how you choose to express your word.

Now go express yourself!

Do you remember the lunchbox thermos? OK, how about lunchboxes? Lunch? Lunchbox thermoses were the de facto standard for transporting liquid refreshment to school, work, anywhere that such refreshment would be needed. The lunchbox thermos would fit perfectly in the lunchbox, and would be blazoned with whatever character design adorned the lunchbox itself. Usually made of plastic, the lunchbox thermos had a screw-top lid, and then a second topper that doubled as a cup, complete with handle. The beauty of the lunchbox thermos was that it kept things hot AND cold, depending on what you needed. Somehow, it just knew. Alas, modern packaging has rendered our old friend obsolete these days. Water in plastic bottles, fruit punch in aluminum pouches, milk in cardboard cartons with straws. The lunchbox thermos just can't compete anymore. Your task today is to put our old friend down. Come up with ten alternative uses for the old lunchbox thermos.

I Didn't Know I Had It In Me

Look around your environment right now. Go ahead. Now, find a noun. Make it random. The randomer the better (Did we just say "randomer?") You got one? Good. Now, take out a piece of paper. Write that word at the top. Now in a stream of conciousness way, without stopping, write fifty words that come to mind when you think of that word. Just start writing, don't stop. Don't evaluate the answers, don't erase anything, just start writing until you have fifty words that come to mind when you think of your word. This makes an excellent brainstorming technique to get ideas out of your head quickly, things that you can refer back to during a project to find associations that might not have come to the forefront had you not rid yourself of the ideas up front.

Top Dog

We love our dogs. Sometimes, more than our kids. Kidding! But we do love our dogs a lot. We'd do anything for them. We spend thousands of dollars on vet visits, food, even outside lodging. It's the lodging we're going to address today. Max out there wants new digs. He says he gives you love and affection and licks and scares away that snot-nosed… errr… wonderful neighbor kid next door. **He also wants you to recognize that he has style.** He can't get his waggle on with that Cocker Spaniel across the street in a crib that's straight rank, aaiight? Your task today is to create the ultimate dog house. Spare no expense. Create a flat so amazing, inside and out, Max will be beatin' the Spaniels away with a chew toy. Trick it out, all the luxuries. Everything Max deserves. Then, when you get thrown out, you'll have someplace to crash. If he lets you. Priorities and all.

Scott "Tired of Bein'" Poe Called For You

Nicknames are sweet. A good nickname will follow a person their entire life. How many people have walked up to Magic Johnson and called him "Earvin?" Nicknames define us. In most cases, we get our nicknames from other people. ***Rarely do we give ourselves nicknames. Unless you're a pro wrestler… then, our apologies.*** Your task today is to give your immediate posse nicknames. If you have co-workers around you, then give them their nicknames. If you don't, choose your circle of friends. The key is that the nicknames have to go with either their first name or their last name. For instance, baseball player Barry Bonds might be Barry "Bail" Bonds. Or moviestar George Clooney might be George "Of the Jungle" Clooney. And don't forget your nickname. You pro wrestler you.

Shoot, I Pulled the Door Off Again!

We're all familiar with super heroes, aren't we?! We all have our favorites, from Superman to Batman to Wonder Woman to the X-Men, we all have that super hero we think is best. But how do we define best? What super hero possesses the greatest super power? What super hero possesses the super power YOU would most like to have? That's your task, to determine which super hero has the power you would most like to have, and then to sketch or list what you would do with that one super power. Would it be flight? How about super strength? And what would that client meeting be like if you could have X-ray vision! You decide. **What's the greatest super power?**

I TRIED IT

Trevor Gerhard, San Clemente, CA

"Let me just say that the word 'exercise' frightened me a bit at first. I didn't want to pull a hammy or anything. So I started by listing a few superheroes that were most familiar on the board in our conference room. Just the classics: Superman, Batman, Wonder Woman, The Hulk and Spider-Man. During one of our Monday briefings I had people call out the super powers for each. When I felt like there were enough, we discussed which were least significant and crossed them off one by one. There was lots of discussion. Some of it got pretty heated. ***It turned out to be a simple but very useful method of group discussion and critique.*** We plan on doing exercises like these every Monday morning. Which was the 'best' super power? Flight, of course. Duh."

Life in the Fast Lane!

Often, finding a creative solution simply means looking at what we see every day in a slightly different way. From our work environments to our computer desktops, altering our perspective can lead to creative results. While we spend countless hours in these environments, there's another place many of us spend countless hours observing our surroundings...our cars. Many of us have taken steps to "customize" the interior of our cars to "brighten the view" of something we stare at everyday... the driver's seat. We have pinned up photos of loved ones, created places for our phones and sunglasses to reside, even flower vases! Your task today is to "redesign" or decorate the dashboard and surrounding area of a car's interior. But not for you... Choose one of these occupational audiences:

cowboy
doctor
park ranger
kindergarten teacher
mortician
actor or actress
creative director
circus clown
pilot

Consider what "things" these occupations might need, and how traveling from one place to the other can be enhanced with your new design. Keep in mind they still need to be able to steer somehow, but the rest is up to you.

Where's This Going?

Where's this going? Stories are the backbone of communication. The art of storytelling often gets lost in creative communication today, taking a back seat to pretty pictures or special effects. Truth is, a good story can take you places even the most sophisticated visual imagery can't take you. We're going to tell a story today, but with a twist. You're going to need at least one other person for this exercise, and if you can find them, four participants would be ideal. You're going to write a "team" story. You start by writing a line of introduction, then hand it off to the next participant, who reads your line, then writes the next line. NO LEADING! Let the next person take the story wherever they like. You simply react to what you've read and add a sentence, then pass it on. Do this until a standard piece of notebook paper is full, then read the story aloud. You might be surprised at where it takes you!

That Penguin is Throwing Up on My Pants

Fire hydrants are cool. *Unless you didn't see it on the street and ran into it with your bike. But that's another story. Fire hydrants are cool, but they're bland. They serve one purpose: to provide water to a fire truck if need be. Some have used it to create a much needed summer oasis of urban-style water fun, but its intended purpose is to help extinguish fires. Typically, fire hydrants are red or yellow, making them fairly apparent to an oncoming fire truck (but seemingly invisible to an unsuspecting bicyclist.) Your task today is to give that fire hydrant a new face. Create a new look for the fire hydrant based on its current design.* You can't change the way the fire hydrant is built, only how it is painted. The structural design must remain intact. *Evaluate its shape, and paint something new on the fire hydrant.*

A Little Dab'll Do Ya!

Commercial jingles are intended to make you remember the product for which the jingle was written. Catchy hooks, short, memorable lines that stick in your head like tar keep that product in the forefront of your mind. When you hit the retail outlet, that inescapable chorus will drive you to purchase the item simply to relieve the insanity. **Bet you have one in your head right now, don't you?** Sorry about that. To help rid you of that insufferable verse, your task today is to create a commercial jingle, but not for something usually in need of a jingle. Your songworthy item is a ball of lint. That stuff that accumulates at the bottom of your pockets, that's right. Create a catchy jingle that will make even the staunchest of lint-haters see the light. Think catchy!

My New Shoes Are Stuck In The ATM

Is there a more convenient way to access our money than the ATM? Before ATMs, we had to wait until the bank opened to access our money. That's so 1967. Since 1968, we've been able to walk up to a number of locations and access our accounts. Some banks have even begun providing other services through the ATM, like selling stamps. What if the ATM could sell more than just stamps? Your task today is to list ten things that an ATM could sell via the standard machine we have today. Consider the size of the machine, and what types of items the current system could accommodate. Along with the purchasing of products, write down ten services the next-generation ATM could sell.

Is This How Milton and Bradley Started?

Here's the scene: You have six kids in your second grade classroom. You're not sure how you got from your cozy chair tucked neatly behind a full screen of Photoshop palettes to standing in front of six seven-year-olds, but that's another story. **The kids have been chanting.** In unison. "Game. Game. Game. Game…" You look around to your horror to find not one, single, solitary board game of any kind. Not a puzzle, not a computer, not even a place to hide for "hide and seek." You are going to have to invent a game out of what you have in the room. And fast. The natives are getting restless. Here's what you have:

A roll of duct tape.
A small rubber ball the size of a bowling ball.
Three shoe boxes.
A broom.
A box of action figures.
A library of hardcover children's books.
The class turtle, "Robbie."
A box of marbles.

Create a game for the six kids out of what you have.

Good luck. Recess is in three hours.

And It Still Staples

The beauty of mechanical devices is that they have so many parts. Why is that beautiful? Because all those parts provide a wealth of interesting forms and shapes and functions. We're going to investigate those forms and shapes and functions a little today. Look around your environment to find something mechanical that someone isn't going to freak about when you take it apart. Now, take that object apart. (If you can't take anything apart, find an object that is as complex as possible in terms of visible parts.) Once you have that item apart, spread the pieces out on your desk. Now, on a piece of sketch paper, use the parts and shapes to create a robot by drawing out the form of the robot on the sketch paper. Only use shapes and parts that you see to make the robot. You can use parts more than once, and they can be used in any arrangement that you can physically see or create. The only thing you can't do is alter the piece to fit your drawing; the pieces must stay true to their original form. Good luck putting it back together, too!

Do These Shorts Make My Line Look Big?

What is the de facto alternative for drawing people? That's right… stick figures. Everyone can draw stick
figures. They are universal. But as versatile as they are, they are equally void of character. Hair can be
drawn, giving them some character, maybe a dress to differentiate sex, but little else is given to our
mono-torsoed friends to tell us WHO they are. Your task today is to attempt to do just that. Look
around you and identify five people. If there is no one around you, picture family members or
friends. Think about the unique attributes these people have that make them… well, them.
Now, draw standard stick figures for each of them, then add one or two unique
characteristics to that stick figure that would identify that particular person. After
you've completed the group, show someone else familiar with the group and
see if they can identify the stick figures as the individuals. And keep
it clean! We know what you were thinking.

Shame on you.

What Time Is It?

We're all familiar with how to tell time. Big hand, little hand, seconds, minutes, hours, A.M. and P.M. Learning to tell time is a right of passage for any first grader, but what if time doesn't really look like what we think? What if numbers don't best represent time? Your task today is to create an alternative to the modern rotary clock. Consider another method to tracking the passing of time. The only restriction is that you can't use numbers in your new time-tracking method. Better get started, you're running out of time… or are you?

Where's That Copy of Emoticons Illustrated?

The mind doesn't think in abstracts. The mind assigns images to abstract ideas, like emotions. Your task today is to fuel that practice by finding images your mind will agree with. Either grab a stack of magazines that can be cannibalized or get online. Find at least five images that express the following emotions:

Angry
Sad
Joyous
Uninspired
Scared

Look for images that your mind would associate with the individual emotion. Cut the images out of the magazine or download the images from the web and print. Create a collage on a sheet of paper of the five images for each emotion.

The Pet Rock Just Got Booted

Introducing "Stick!" Stick is the hottest new toy on the market. Kids love Stick. They can't get enough Stick. Stick sells millions of units every month. **It's sweeping the nation!** At least it will when you and your marketing machine convince them it is. Forget that it's really just a common stick that you would find at the base of any tree—you need to create the campaign that introduces the world to "Stick!" Use any marketing or advertising methods you think best could sell "Stick!" to every kid on the planet. Consider possible uses, applications and fun-loving tricks and tips.

I'll Take the Next Catapult, Thanks

The choices are clear. If you are on one floor of a building, and you want to get to another floor, you're left with either the stairs, an elevator, an escalator, some form of ramp, perhaps a fire pole, the occasional ladder or a jump. That's it. But since we're living in the world of "what if?" today, imagine none of those were invented yet. What system, other than the ones listed above, could you devise to get people from one floor to the next safely? Consider both getting up and getting down. Safety is key, too. No pushing folks to their deaths from forty floors up!

Interview With Mike Dietz

The mind of an illustrator is a fascinating place. The ability to illustrate any image that comes to mind is a powerful, artistic communication force. **What makes it twice as amazing is when the illustrator in question doubles as an animator.** Now that mind goes from fascinating to downright frightening. Welcome to Mike Dietz. Illustrator. Animator. Designer. Mike does it all, and although we've never been up in there, we suspect his mind develops pictures and scenarios we can only dream of.

If you asked him (and we did) Mike wouldn't characterize himself as an illustrator or animator or even a designer. Mike would call himself a storyteller. "Animation and illustration deal heavily in story," Mike begins. "Animation tells a story across a linear timeline, while illustration implies a story by offering a view of a single moment in time. *Of the two, implying a story with that single image is much more challenging and rewarding when you get it right. It also allows more participation from the viewer, since a single image can be interpreted in many ways."*

As a Mind-For-Hire guy, Mike gets the privilege, and challenge, of both working in large teams of creatives as well as one-man projects. One would think maintaining a high level of creative thought would be difficult with all those variables. ***"The best part about animation is the collaborative nature of the work,"*** Mike explains, "while the best part about illustration is the opportunity to work alone. If that sounds contradictory, well that's because it is. Each has its advantages and disadvantages, and I feel lucky that I get to experience both sides of the equation. Obviously, working as a part of a larger team offers constant creative stimulus from your other team members, and the results are, and should be, greater than what you could create on your own. However, the tradeoff is relinquishing creative control over certain aspects of the project, and unless the project has a strong leader, you can easily end up with designed-by-committee mediocrity. Conversely, illustration, like other single-creator endeavors, offers the artistic potency of a single creative voice, which can be extremely satisfying for both the creator and the viewer. The big pitfall, however, is you can often end up creating in a vacuum, sitting alone in your studio with little guidance or feedback. It's important to get out there, talking to other artists and looking at their work, so you don't become a creative hermit."

And what about creativity? What is creativity to a guy that can literally reenact any scenario he can dream up with characters he draws and situations he creates? "Creativity, by definition, is simply the ability to create," Mike says. "But what we're really talking about is expressing ourselves through original thoughts and ideas, arriving at unique solutions to problems by approaching those problems in fresh, unexpected ways. Creativity, and how to harness it, is an elusive subject. It comes from deep inside you and is molded by the sum of your life experiences, so the process is very personal and unique. It resides most powerfully in our subconscious, which means to best tap into it we have to relinquish conscious control over the process—something some people have a difficult time with. You have to trust the process, let it come to you. Just make sure you have a pencil and paper nearby, because sometimes the best ideas can be the most fleeting."

You would think a guy like Mike has very little trouble coming up with ideas, but like any creative, idea generation is a process for Mike. "Preparing for creativity is really constantly exposing yourself to creative influences, overloading your brain with stimulus to keep your subconscious always working and processing information. That can mean watching films, looking at artwork, listening to music, reading books, drawing from life, walking in the woods—whatever. That's the raw material you collect and draw from when the deadline is looming and the client is screaming."

And from a guy who has worked on some major network animated shows, movie and gaming credits, as well as some of the largest corporate entities on the face of the planet, the power of the idea doesn't get lost in the process.

"Ideas are the real currency in our business. Without a good idea, all the artistic proficiency in the world is just window dressing. You can tell a good story with crappy animation and it'll still tug at your heart, but the best animation in the world won't save a bad story."

Can you tell that to my client, Mike?

Mike Dietz
Slappy Pictures
www.slappypictures.com

Does This Dress Make My Brain Look Fat?

Ahhhh, dress-up. Who doesn't like dress-up? Put your hands down. Well, your brain likes dress-up, and so,we must give your brain the confidence it needs to be who it is. Go to **www.wakeupmybrain.com/cftcm/exercises/dressup.html** and download and print the file named "MyBrain.pdf." These are your brains. Naked. Nude. Unclothed. They need clothes. But not just any clothes. You need to draw over these brains with garb that would make them feel at home in:

A Baseball Dugout
A Psychiatric Ward
A Deserted Island
A Kung-Fu Tournament
A Design Firm
A Graveyard

Feel free to add whatever accessory or flair needed to set 'em off right!

Don't Put This on Your Hood Though

Every car manufacturer has an emblem. Not necessarily a logo, but an emblem. It adorns the front and back of each car they make. Volkswagen, for instance, has the VW emblem. BMW has the circle with the white and blue quadrants, and Ford has the blue oval with their name written in script inside. Wouldn't it be cool if we were identified by our emblem? That's your task today. Create an emblem for yourself. Not a logo, but an emblem. It can have something to do with your name, your initials, or a nickname—anything that that says who you are. Remember, it just has to look cool in chrome.

Wave 'Em Proud

Flags are identifiers we are all familiar with, from countries to states to counties to even sports teams. Flags address the viewer with the colors and the meaning and the stature and the pride. Flags represent something. Everything should have a flag. Let's work on that today. Your challenge today is to create the official flag for one of the following entities:

Dog Chew Toys United
Computer Programmers Club
Weightlifting Nuns of America
Pizza Delivery Association
Poker Players' Diet Group

Use colors, shapes, imagery, whatever you like. Design your flag and fly it high!

You're Fired!

Donald Trump made that cobra-like hand gesture during his TV show *The Apprentice* when he fired someone from the show. You know the hand gesture. Put your arm up to about eye level, bend your knuckles forward, like you're going to poke someone's eye out with all four fingers, then say **"You're Fired!"** and do the poking motion very sharply. That felt kinda good, huh? Now, when someone makes that motion, they don't even have to say the words, people know what it means. What if we had other hand motions for other common terms? That's your task today, to create hand motions for the following scenarios:

That font sucks!
Where are we going for lunch today?
I can't stay late, I'm sick.
Make it look clean and uncluttered.
Is the web down?

Create these hand gestures, then share them with your friends and co-workers so you can save those precious words for some other sentence.

I Wouldn't Have Chosen Relish for the Carpet, But That's Just Me

We're pretty familiar with construction materials. We know what a roof shingle feels like, or the smell of fresh paint on the walls. We've also seen houses built out of other materials, like gingerbread. Shorter scale, of course, but tastes way better than real houses. We've heard. What if we had to build a house out of materials that might seem less construction-esque? Like condiments? That's your task today. If you had to build a house, gingerbread-house scale, out of common grocery store condiments, what would you make? What would the walls be made from, or the roof? What about the walkway? Think of anything you would put on any sandwich, burger, hot dog, BBQ, anything you would use as a topping of any form.

Ya, that's messy!

Where'd They Get THAT?!

You're going to need one other willing soul for this exercise. Get a paper bag (or anything that can carry a few items without being seen). Give the bag to the other participant and ask him or her to fill the bag with four random items. The only restriction is that the items have to be able to fit entirely in the bag. When your partner is done, have them roll the bag up so you can't see the contents and give it back to you. These are your "clues." The story is that you were having coffee at a cafe down the street, and a man ran up to you and gave you this bag. He said "I can't explain now, but I need you to hold this bag for me. I'm being chased by three men, I think they are government agents, but I'm not sure. Please take this bag for me, I'll contact you later." He then looked behind him anxiously and ran off. You took the bag back to your office and even though it's probably not a good idea, you decide the mystery is too great to stand. You have to know this guy's story. Now take the bag and remove the contents onto your desk or table. The four objects you see are your only clues to the mystery of who this guy is, who he was running from and what's going on. Write a story about how these four objects go together, who the guy was and the story behind his mysterious circumstances.

What Does SHE over THERE Have To Do With THAT?

Three separate things. They don't have anything to do with each other… at least on the surface. They are random. Individual. Unassociated. Until you come along. Grab a digital camera and take three pictures: One of a stranger. The second of a place. The third, a random object. Print out the photos. Your task today is to write a short story, a couple paragraphs at the most, of what these three random photographs have in common. Tell a story of who the person is, how the place plays into the person, and what the object means to the story.

I'm Gonna Need a Bigger Fishbowl!

There are over 25,000 types of fish in the world. That's a lot of fish. Each one looks slightly different than the other, even within the same species. Some fish are amazingly beautiful and relatively harmless, some are scary, mean and downright dangerous. Each has its defense mechanisms from the food chain entry immediately above them. What if you could create your own fish? That's your task today. Create your own fish, its shape, its color, its defense mechanisms, what it eats, how it swims, everything you can think of about a fish. Make it your own. And stay away from the sushi until you're done.

The Envelope, Please

Award season for the entertainment industry gets crazy, with the top players carrying home serious hardware. Gold statues, trophies and crystal plaques are handed to the best of the best. Suffice to say, we'll probably never walk home with an Oscar, but that's not our world. **What would we walk home with?**

Your challenge today is to create the award for your place of employment or your household. What would it be called? What symbol would it represent? What would the categories be that someone might be eligible for? Create your mantelpiece treasure and then give one to yourself, in the category of **"Best-Creative-Exercise-Doer-Person,"** or something.

I Never Knew So Much About a Pencil Sharpener

Look around your area right now. Choose one object that you see. The reality of the way that object came to be in your area probably wouldn't make an intriguing story. That's where you come in. You're going to create the story of that object, the made-up story of the history of that particular object, and how it came into your possession. Leave "reality" behind and create something that could have been true, but most likely is far more fantasy than reality.

What Does Melancholy Look Like?

Our minds do not think in abstracts. The mind assigns imagery to every abstract subject it needs to process. Try it: What do you think of when you hear the word "honesty?" You pictured something, didn't you? We use these same images to communicate. If our client wants to convey the sense of honesty to a group of their consumers, there are images we can use to achieve that abstract idea. Your task today is to write down the first thing you think of when you hear the following abstract words:

Rage
Order
Justice
Evil
Peace
God
History
Pain
Smart

We Got The Beat!

It's a great feeling when you get in "the zone" with your work. You're just cranking out the ideas or the production or the design, you're really flowing. They call that getting in a rhythm. If we could bottle that rhythm and save it for the days we simply can't get on track, we could sell it on eBay and retire. Although getting in the rhythm is something we can't schedule or predict, we CAN work on rhythm itself. This will work best if you can get multiple people to participate—the more the better. We're going to work out a little rhythm synergy. Start by creating a simple beat, whether by stomping your feet, clapping your hands, pounding your desk, whatever. Keep it simple and steady and even. Next, get another participant to create another beat that is in time with yours, but is a different cadence. Then, another participant joins in at the same time but with something new, whether that's a different beat or using a different object to create the beat. Do this one participant at a time until everyone is in the groove. Keep it steady for a few beats, then when you're ready, call out "4, 3, 2, 1, BAM!" in time with your beat and everyone stops. Wanna get everyone on the same page during the day? Office beats will do the trick every time!

Black Eye Bart's a-Lookin' For Ya!

Every sprouting town back in the Old West seemed to have that black-hatted, black-vested, scruffy villain-type character that would bust into the local saloon and start causin' a ruckus. Inevitably, someone would either get shot, thrown through the saloon window, tossed over the counter or end up outside in the trough. As the creative-minded sheriff, you've had just about enough of this ornery pole-cat, so you've decided to create a trap in the saloon to capture his hide and scat that dubious gunslinger right to the jail-house. Your task today is to devise a plan to capture said villain without finishing him off, and without him sending anybody in the bar to the undertaker!

Poor Hamster... Never Had a Chance

Street signs have a design all their own. The challenge is to design something that communicates to everyone, regardless of language or culture. We are all familiar with street signs and their direction, but what if you had to design a series of street signs for something unusual? That is your task. Design a street sign for the following situations:

No Applying Makeup or Shaving While Riding a Tricycle

Donuts Ahead

No Throwing Hamsters

Stop if You Want

Clothing Optional

"For this exercise, I designed five wild street signs. One included 'no putting on lipstick or shaving while on a tricycle.' Making these signs really worked my mental muscles. I had to think outside the box in order to come up with a creative solution. Although I only spent fifteen minutes on the signs

I could have spent hours.

It was hard to think of it as a short, fun project rather than an extensive one because that is what we designers do all day—really focus on serious projects. It was good for me to do something with no pressure just to get my creative juices flowing. I really enjoyed the fun and short aspect of this exercise, but it could be fun one day to take it seriously and put the signs all over a city for an art project."

Margaret Minnis, Lake Forest, CA

I Call It "Helveticaslon"

Fonts are as important a part of visual communication as any other visual element. Fonts convey tone and communicate mood just like color or composition. A font chosen poorly can damage the message of an otherwise effective design. As graphic elements, fonts are beautiful forms, unique to themselves, carrying characteristics from one letter to another that identifies it with its family. But what happens when two fonts from the opposite ends of town hook up at a party, have a little too much to drink, then end up married with offspring the next day? It happens. Your challenge today is to take two fonts from opposite ends of the spectrum and combine them to make one font. Do so by choosing a letter of the alphabet, then fusing the two versions of that letter to create a version that retains the identifying characteristics of both fonts. You can do this digitally or you can draw the new letter on a sketchpad. Name your new font something that identifies both fonts. Feel free to do the same to each letter of the alphabet until you've created your own complete font. And break out the baby powder and font diapers.

How Do You Photograph Smelly?

If someone told you to grab a digital camera and shoot a picture of a pencil, you'd know exactly what to do, wouldn't you? You'd find a pencil and photograph it. Pretty straightforward. But what if someone told you to take a picture of "bored." Now what do you shoot? No, not yourself. Very funny. You would have to first give "bored" a physical feature, then find something that represented that feature. Your task is to do just that, but with a twist. Choose one of the words below and take sixteen digital photographs that characterize the word:

flight
think
aggressive
joy
successful
tedious
loud

Think of the personification of the word as well as the abstract concept of the meaning. And feel free to take a picture of this book. It seems to satisfy them all!

Twinkies Count As Two

Sometimes, we just have to disconnect from reality for a moment and live in fantasy land. Some of us get mail there, but that's another story. Your task today is to imagine that you have accidentally fallen off the cruise ship on your way to the Bahamas, and you've washed ashore on a small, deserted island. The funny thing was you had a premonition the night before that you were going to do exactly that, and you had the clarity of mind to take three items with you when you fell overboard. **What are the three items you would take with you and why?**

Should Bees Wear Kneepads?

Phrases and idioms are sometimes confusing. Meant to provide some form of meaning to a situation by associating it with something known, idioms often shed little light on anything unless the meaning of the saying is known to all. Your task today is to provide meaning to five popular sayings, whether you know the real origin or not. Take the five sayings below and write where you think they came from:

Throwing the baby out with the bathwater
The whole nine yards
The real McCoy
Raining cats and dogs
The bee's knees

If you don't know the actual meaning of one of the sayings, that's OK, don't quit, just make one up. You don't need to throw the baby out with the bathwater!

I Can't Come In, I Have The Gout

There are certain days that you just can't go in to work. You have tickets to the day game, the amusement park is half off today, your buddy is treating for a round of golf, whatever the reason, you just can't go in. But you also know that you can't call up and say you have something better to do today, so you need an excuse. "Cough, cough," ain't gonna cut it—you work with creatives. They expect more. And you need to give it to them. List your top ten creative excuses to get out of work. "The alarm didn't go off" doesn't make the cut.

I Can't Spell "Abnormal Martian" with Just Seven Characters!

Every project we do carries certain restrictions. Whether those are based on budget, talent, medium, production… **Restrictions are a fact of design.** Sometimes, those restrictions come in the form of rules. Rules like, "You only have seven characters to use to communicate a message." Let's use that one today. License plates are seven characters at the most. You can use less, but not more. Your task today is to create the vanity license plate for the following people:

A Nun
A Gambler
A Yarn Store Clerk
A Waitress at a Biker Bar
A Thrill Seeker/Adrenaline Junkie
A TV Game Show Host
A Pizza Delivery Guy

Feel free to create the license plate frame along with the vanity plates. Throw in a bumper sticker if you're feeling adventurous. ROKNRLL!

Like, Ummm... I Mean, It's Like...

The sense of smell is a powerful "rememberer." Imagine if we had no sense of smell. That's your challenge today. Take out a sheet of paper and describe your favorite smell. Doesn't sound too hard, right? Well, not so fast. You have to do it without using the words "like" or "as."

So much for starting that sentence with, "It smells like," huh?

Yes Doc, I think I Broke My Pancreas Sleeping

Most team sports have some form of physical contact that's part of the game. Some sports are all about the contact. And a few are considered "full contact" ***sports, as the participants pound each other throughout the competition. While these sports are fun to watch, they generally hurt to play, so the general masses turn to less violent activities. Until those activities suddenly become*** "full contact!" ***Your task today is to list ten games, sports or activities that, simply put, should convert to "full contact." "Checkmate"... BOOM!... ("Medic!")***

Tweety Would Freak!

You've just won the National Birdhouse Design Grant. Didn't even know you applied, did you? The grant gives you exactly $5000 to spend on the design and construction of the world's greatest birdhouse. It's your task today to figure out what you would build. Consider the applications, both inside and outside, and how the birdhouse would be introduced to its new tenants.

Trick or Pantone Book?

Trick or Pantone Book?
It's Halloween, and you've decided to go as one of the following occupations:

Graphic Designer
Illustrator
Photographer
Art Director
Musician
Writer

What would your costume look like for each of these characters? Consider those you know and the stereotypes you've grown accustomed to assigning to each.

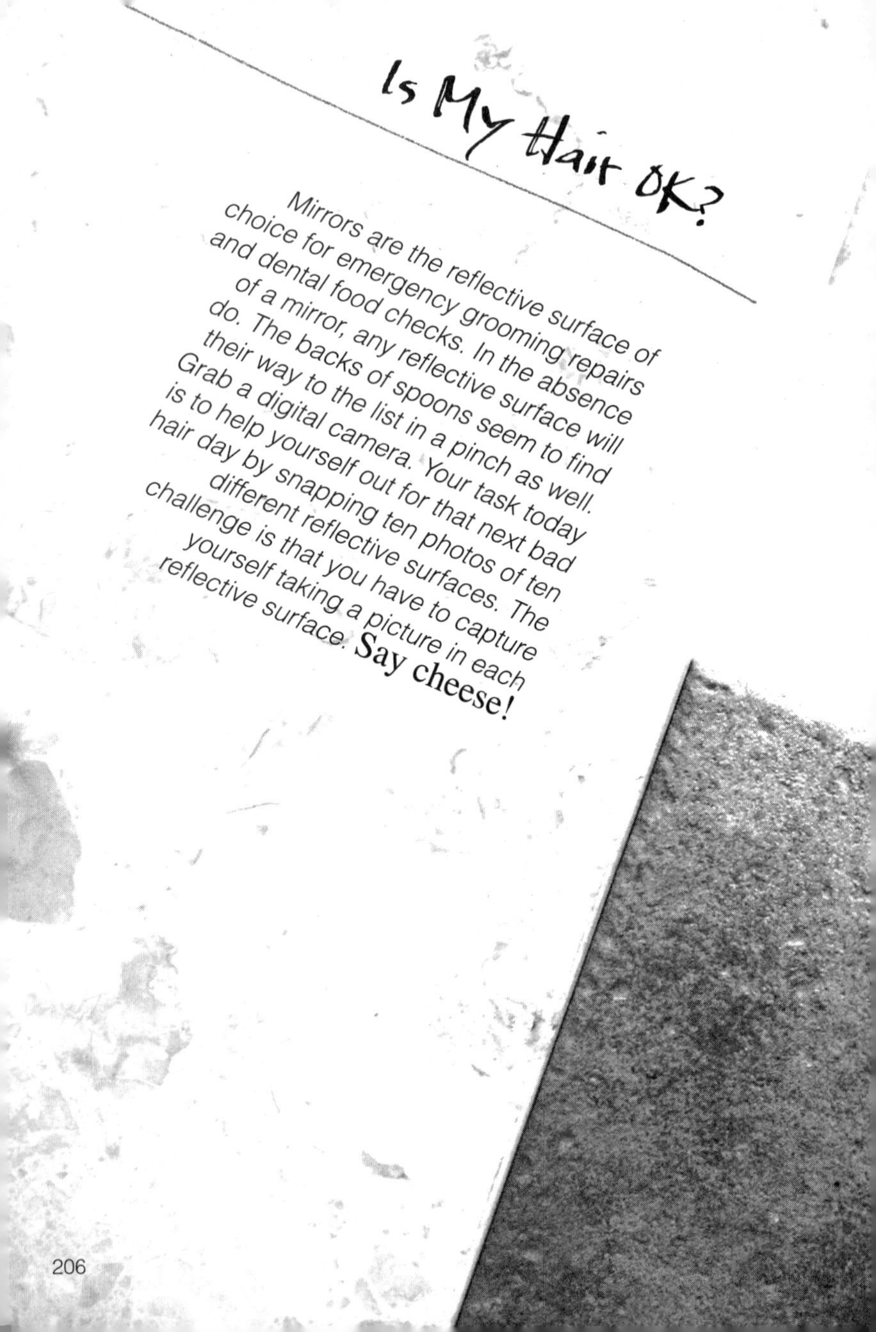

Is My Hair OK?

Mirrors are the reflective surface of choice for emergency grooming repairs and dental food checks. In the absence of a mirror, any reflective surface will do. The backs of spoons seem to find their way to the list in a pinch as well. Grab a digital camera. Your task today is to help yourself out for that next bad hair day by snapping ten photos of ten different reflective surfaces. The challenge is that you have to capture yourself taking a picture in each reflective surface. Say cheese!

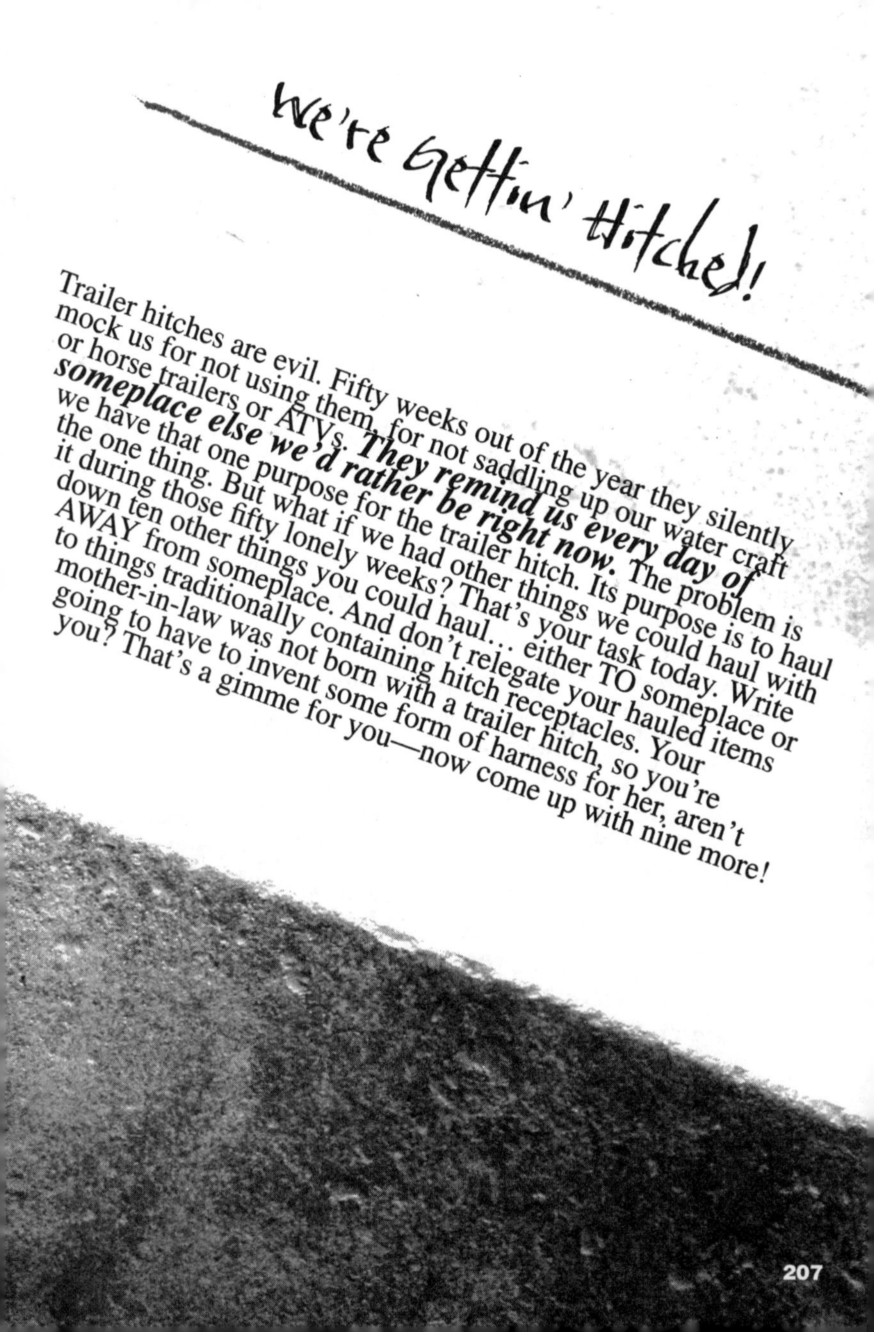

We're Gettin' Hitched!

Trailer hitches are evil. Fifty weeks out of the year they silently mock us for not using them, for not saddling up our water craft or horse trailers or ATVs. ***They remind us every day of someplace else we'd rather be right now.*** The problem is we have that one purpose for the trailer hitch. Its purpose is to haul the one thing. But what if we had other things we could haul with it during those fifty lonely weeks? That's your task today. Write down ten other things you could haul… either TO someplace or AWAY from someplace. And don't relegate your hauled items to things traditionally containing hitch receptacles. Your mother-in-law was not born with a trailer hitch, so you're going to have to invent some form of harness for her, aren't you? That's a gimme for you—now come up with nine more!

Did You Just Get Really, Really Mad At That Bank Robber?

Actor/comedian Ben Stiller starred in a movie adaptation of the Dark Horse comic book legendary series *Mystery Men*, where he banded together with other "ordinary" people who thought they had super hero powers, but in reality, their powers were average at best. One member of the team could throw a bowling ball extremely accurately, one used targeted flatulence to disarm the evil doers, and Stiller's character would get really, really mad. That was it. He didn't have any special power outside of getting really, really mad. These "super heroes" would bumble their way into bad situations, eventually getting rescued by "real" super heroes. We're all mystery men in some way, aren't we? Your task today is to create your personal "Mystery Men" team of average super heroes. These can be people you know or completely made-up characters, but you should create four to five "heroes" and explain their "average" super powers. You can probably leave the flatulence to The S h p l e e e n !

AlohaMobile

Everyone loves Hawaii! And what's not to love? White sand beaches, pineapple fu-fu drinks with umbrellas, the clear, blue ocean. Even the graphic style of Hawaii is attractive. The Polynesian visual language is unique and distinctive, with certain graphic elements consistent through many applications. There are certain places we expect to see that distinctive Polynesian style, and some, it turns out, we don't. Today we're going to explore the places we don't. Your task is to choose one of the following "places" and recreate it, Hawaiian style:

An Automobile
Your Desk Area
An Outhouse
A Doghouse
A Dump Truck

Consider what Hawaiian elements can be added to the environment, including graphic prints, foliage or uniquely Polynesian decor. Here's a tip: Don't bend over if you're not wearing anything under that grass skirt!

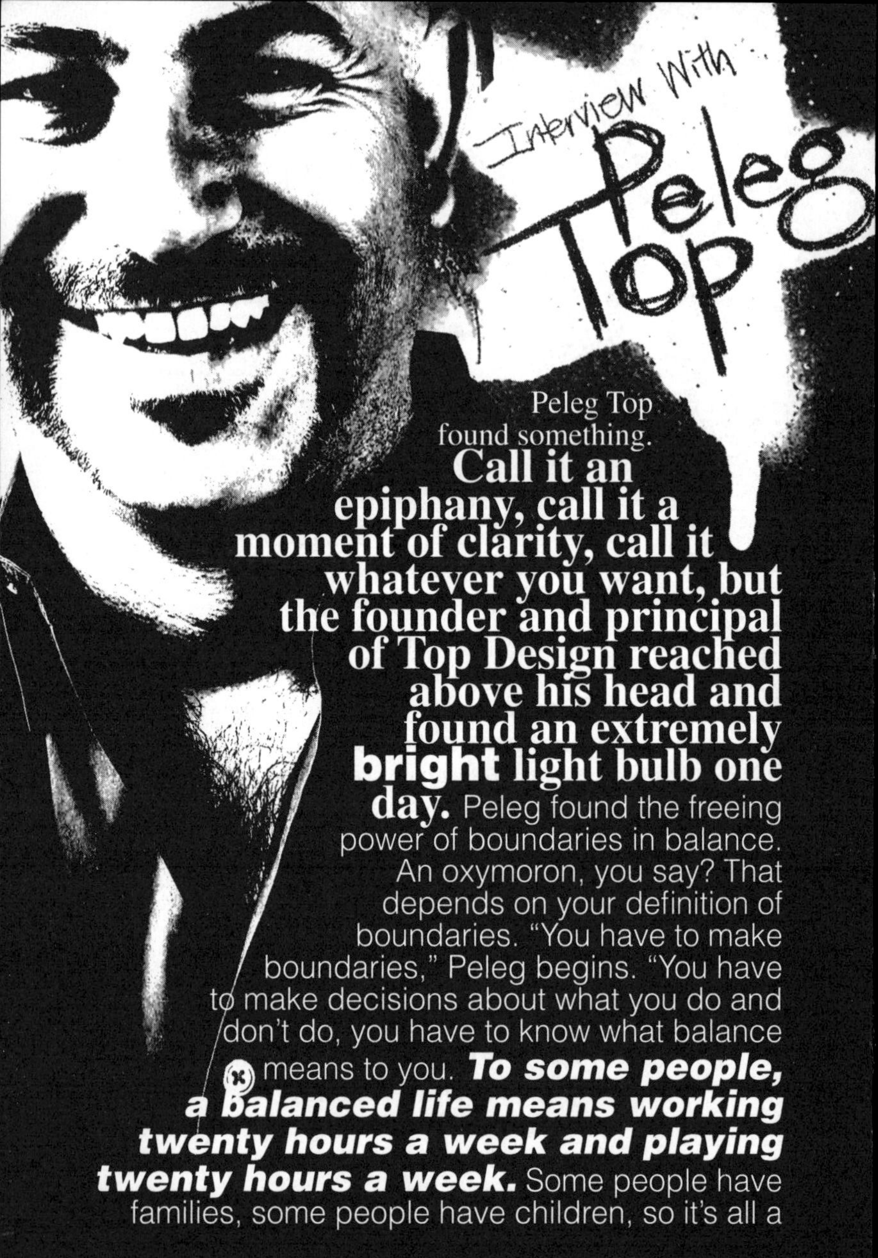

Interview With

Peleg Top

Peleg Top found something. **Call it an epiphany, call it a moment of clarity, call it whatever you want, but the founder and principal of Top Design reached above his head and found an extremely bright light bulb one day.** Peleg found the freeing power of boundaries in balance. An oxymoron, you say? That depends on your definition of boundaries. "You have to make boundaries," Peleg begins. "You have to make decisions about what you do and don't do, you have to know what balance means to you. ***To some people, a balanced life means working twenty hours a week and playing twenty hours a week.*** Some people have families, some people have children, so it's all a matter of priorities and having the time you want to allocate to each activity in your life. Setting boundaries on things is really important—boundaries like how often you check your e-mail, how late you work, what time you stop answering the phone, what days you work or don't work, how many vacations you take a year, what you do to cultivate your creativity, what do you do to ***recharge and inspire yourself.***

I made a decision to take Fridays off because there are so many other things that I'm involved with now. ***On Fridays, I tend to just do fun stuff for me.*** I'll go to a museum or meet a friend and go to the movies or go shopping—just stuff to fuel my soul. And it's different every Friday. Sometimes I'll use Friday to work on my book, or organize photos, or things that are important to me that I want to put the time into. They tend to be a lot slower."

Peleg has had his share of success with his freeing perspective of working a balanced life. He has built his design firm around a foundation of creativity and talent. But contrary to popular belief, that creativity isn't born in the work alone. "Design is not really a way for me to express myself," Peleg says. **"Design is a product that we produce for a client. It's something that a lot of designers don't know how to separate from.** It's not about them—it's about the client. They have the craft to deliver the client what they want. I say keep the self-expression going, but find other avenues—don't just leave it up to your design work. Your design work will improve once you tap into your creativity in other ways. You're not going to find creativity from a computer. You have to be proactive about creativity—you can't just sit there and expect it to come."

So where does Peleg find the fuel behind his idea generation? **"To me, creativity is all about collaboration. I love collaborating with other designers. I see myself almost like a design producer where I bring in the talents that collaborate with me and together we come up with ideas and create things for the projects. Most of the creativity comes when I collaborate. I look for inspiration from that process. That's when magic happens."**

Peleg has found that, along with collaborating with the outside talent he brings on board from project to project, his small internal staff brings fresh, new ideas to the daily brainstorming session that is running a design business. **He has taken to choosing his team carefully—and has given them the tools and freedoms they require to keep the creative fire burning.** *"I sponsor creative classes for my staff," Peleg explains. "So if they're interested in taking a drawing class or a design class, I'll pay for it.*

We brainstorm a lot. *We'll go off and do research by ourselves, generate ideas and then we come together and talk about our ideas. It's very organic. Something usually comes out of it. They're all really inspired people. It's important for me to work with people that have balanced lives."*

And if you imagined a creative visionary like Peleg would take special care in forming his creative environment, you'd be right. "I bought a house! It was a single-family home that we gutted down and redesigned as an office. So we have a full kitchen and we cook here once a week. We all cook together and have lunch. We have a big back yard. It's a nice environment, it's very homey. **People don't feel like they're going to an office. It's a very relaxed environment, like a second home.** It's nice to just sit and relax and read and cook if you need to."

Culinary creativity counts!

Knock Knock!

There is a simple trick to opening and closing a door. Many don't know this, so don't be shocked or alarmed at the impending knowledge you're about to receive. All you have to do is turn the doorknob. Complex indeed. But sometimes, there's no doorknob. Now what? You are forced to use your critical thinking skills to evaluate the bizarre contraption bolted to the door in lieu of the traditional entry method. It's good we're critical thinkers, or else we'd be standing outside that door all day. After evaluation of the entry vehicle, you are sure of one thing: you could do better at designing a doorknob. Good, because that's what you're doing today. Your challenge today is to design your own doorknob. You can either choose to design simply on aesthetics and leave the internal mechanisms to the engineering department, or you can design the entire piece and how it would interact with the door.

Shoot! I Left the Ten Trophy Again!

The sound of the ball return, the smell of the corn dogs, the rush of adrenaline you get when you hit the pocket just perfect and the pins don't just tumble over, they **explode!** Must be the irresistible allure of bowling night. Or in this case, bowling day! Not everyone can take time out of their day to go to the bowling alley and throw a few games, but that doesn't mean you can't bring the games to the office! Your task today is to kick some serious ten-pin butt! Find at least one other competitor, find enough space to use as a lane (hallways are perfect) and create your pins from whatever materials you can find. Each of you needs to find your own "ball," using whatever is available in your environment or even making your own rolling devices out of arts and crafts materials. One acts as the bowler, the other as the "pin-setter-upper." Switch it up every frame, and be sure to practice your fist pump. Loser buys the corn dogs.

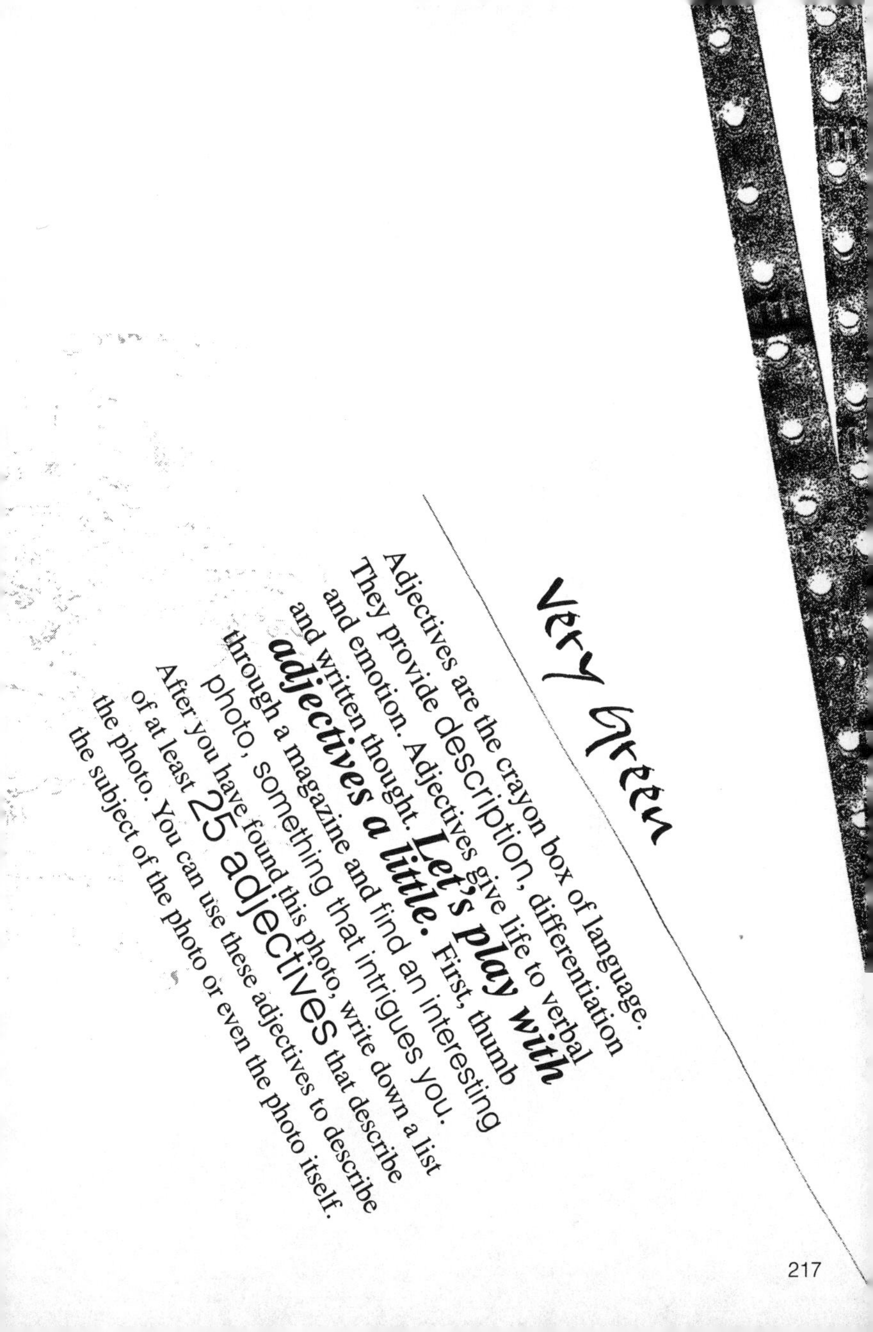

Very Green

Adjectives are the crayon box of language. They provide description, differentiation and emotion. Adjectives give life to verbal and written thought. **Let's play with adjectives a little.** First, thumb through a magazine and find an interesting photo, something that intrigues you. After you have found this photo, write down a list of at least 25 adjectives that describe the photo. You can use these adjectives to describe the subject of the photo or even the photo itself.

Drats

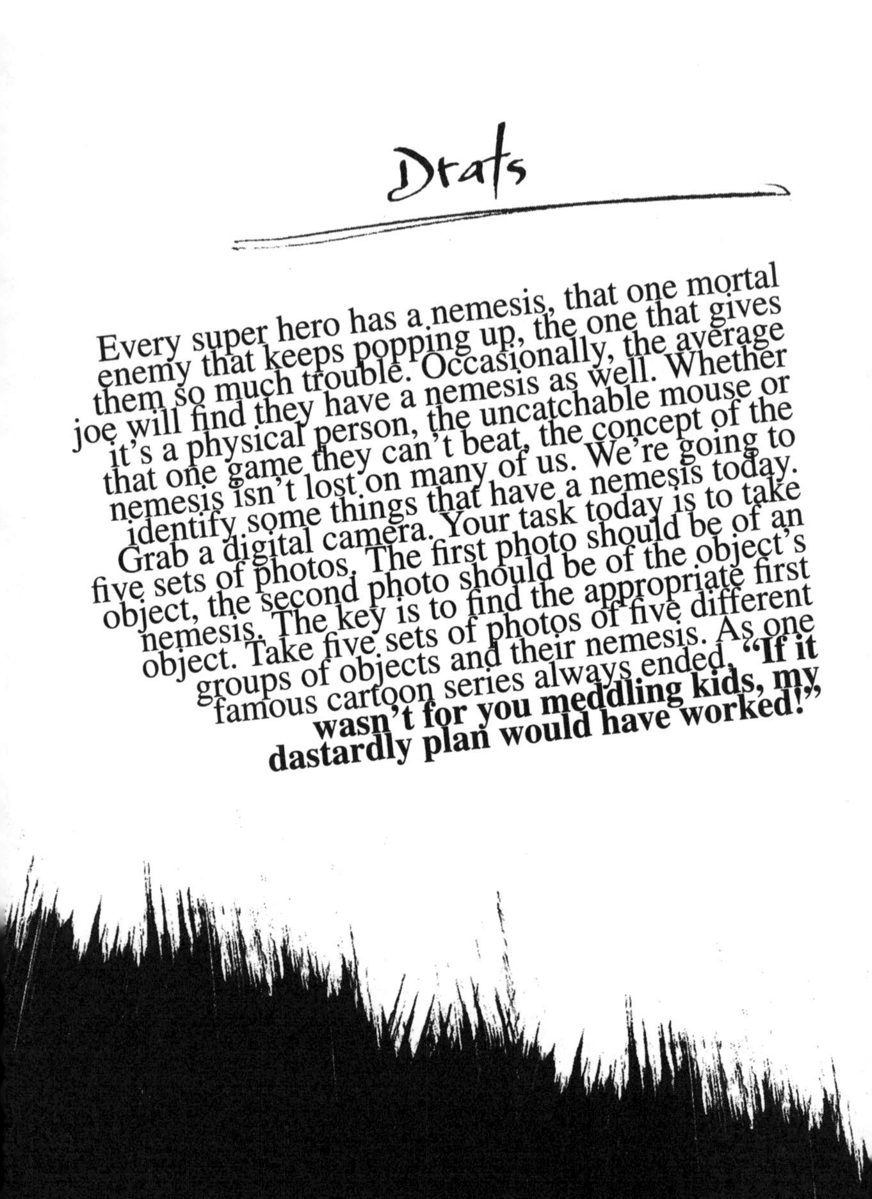

Every super hero has a nemesis, that one mortal enemy that keeps popping up, the one that gives them so much trouble. Occasionally, the average joe will find they have a nemesis as well. Whether it's a physical person, the uncatchable mouse or that one game they can't beat, the concept of the nemesis isn't lost on many of us. We're going to identify some things that have a nemesis today. Grab a digital camera. Your task today is to take five sets of photos. The first photo should be of an object, the second photo should be of the object's nemesis. The key is to find the appropriate first object. Take five sets of photos of five different groups of objects and their nemesis. As one famous cartoon series always ended, **"If it wasn't for you meddling kids, my dastardly plan would have worked!"**

Oh No, They Didn't!

We have laws. When those laws are broken, there are crimes. But what happens when an unwritten law is broken? Unwritten laws are "guidelines" that everyone knows exist, but aren't technically covered in the true law. **Each industry, activity or profession has unwritten laws.** Even individuals have formed their own unwritten laws. When these laws are broken, crimes are commited. People should be punished! Using a particular font might be breaking one of your laws, or perhaps some other form of layout faux pas is high on the list. Whatever the crime, write down the top five crimes of your industry. Write down the punishment for those crimes as well. Flogging not included.

Does That Come In Suede?

There is a truth that is lost in all the political and sociological debate that occurs on a daily basis throughout the world. A truth that is poignant, strong and correct. A truth that, simply put… is true. Creatives get cold, too. There it is. Out in the open for all to hear. Creatives need warm clothing just like everyone else. But we're different… we're special. We don't just want any winter parka, we want something that fits our unique lifestyle. It's as much about application as it is about fashion. Your task is to create such a jacket. Create a jacket for your creative lifestyle. Consider not just materials, but how that jacket fits your everyday needs. Does it have things attached to it you might need? Are there hidden compartments? What's the pocket situation like? Consider what features the new twenty-first century creative's jacket would offer.

I'll Have the BBQ Rack of Vader Please!

Themed restaurants are nothing new. We've dined at establishments that are modeled after our favorite cartoon characters, sports or music genre. But our favorite movie? That's your challenge today. Think of your all-time favorite movie. The one you could quote every line from. Now create a themed restaurant around that movie. Consider the subject of the movie, the characters, the setting. Now, by either writing down the ideas or sketching them out, create the features of the establishment, from the tables and tableware to the costumes to the decoration to the food. Think of as many themed elements as you can for your favorite movie-themed restaurant. Just don't order the veal.

What an Odd Place for a Totem Pole

Quick, name five people you know right now that don't have a cell phone. You can stop now. We couldn't come up with more than two either. The point is, everyone has a cell phone. What that means is that there has to be cell phone service just about everywhere we go. We know this because we see the cell phone towers everywhere. On the street, in backyards, rising in the air like wheat stalks sprouting cell phone panels at the top. Some places are doing their best to hide the cell towers by disguising them as trees or painting them the colors of adjacent buildings. Your task today is to come up with ten other ways to "hide" cell phone towers by either disguising them as something other than a tree or coming up with another way altogether to get those cell phone panels high enough that our call home doesn't get dropped every 100 yards.

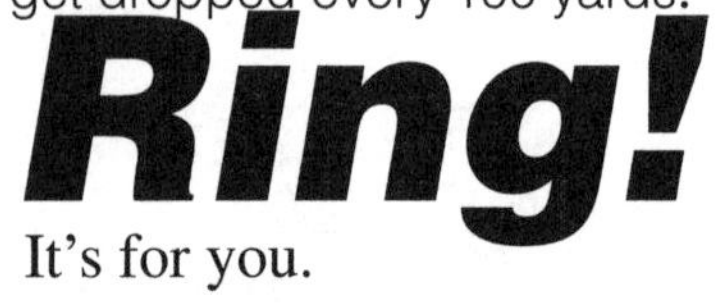

It's for you.

Dumb as a Rock

Play dumb. Right now. Go ahead. Are you dumb yet? Stay that way for a second. There are some questions you should be asked while you are in this state. When asked the questions, write down the dumbest answers or explanation you can think of. Just write one for each. That's one… the number that comes right before two and right after "count from one to ten."

Why do we have feet?
What type of music is the best?
How did they invent macaroni and cheese?
What's your favorite color and why?
Whatcha drinkin'?

Have a Nice Day!

There are clichéd greeting phrases we all have grown accustomed to saying and hearing. When an acquaintance passes you in the hall and says "Hey, how ya doin'?" he rarely wants to know **EXACTLY** how you're doing, stuffy nose and bad date experience included. It's just a phrase, a greeting of sorts. Phone greetings and salutations are similar. "Hello" and "goodbye" are the odds-on favorites, but "Have a nice day!" is gaining ground in the fight for salutation supremacy. The problem with "Have a nice day!" is that it's not personalized for you or the caller. But what if it could be? That's your task today. Create a phone salutation that would be personalized for your business along the lines of "Have a nice day!" It might simply be to replace the word "nice" with something that is more in line with your business or company name. It could be something completely wild and out there. So have at it, and have yourself a truly caffeinated day!

Patti Bacheldor, Atlanta, GA

Lick and Stick

Postage stamps are a normal part of mail delivery. Someone has to pay to have it delivered, don't they? Over the years, postage stamps have been designed to celebrate everything from events and happenings to people and animals. We love postage stamps so much, people even collect them. Today, you're going to get a chance to design your own stamp, only with a twist. Today's challenge is to create a stamp design for one of the following scenarios:

Your work was chosen for a major design award.
Gerbils have overrun the White House.
Peanut Butter and Jelly was elected National Sandwich.
It's official: Christmas comes twice a year now.
Orange is banned from nationally recognized colors.

Your stamp can be any shape or size, but must include a denomination.

That's Great, Moses Is In Foul Trouble

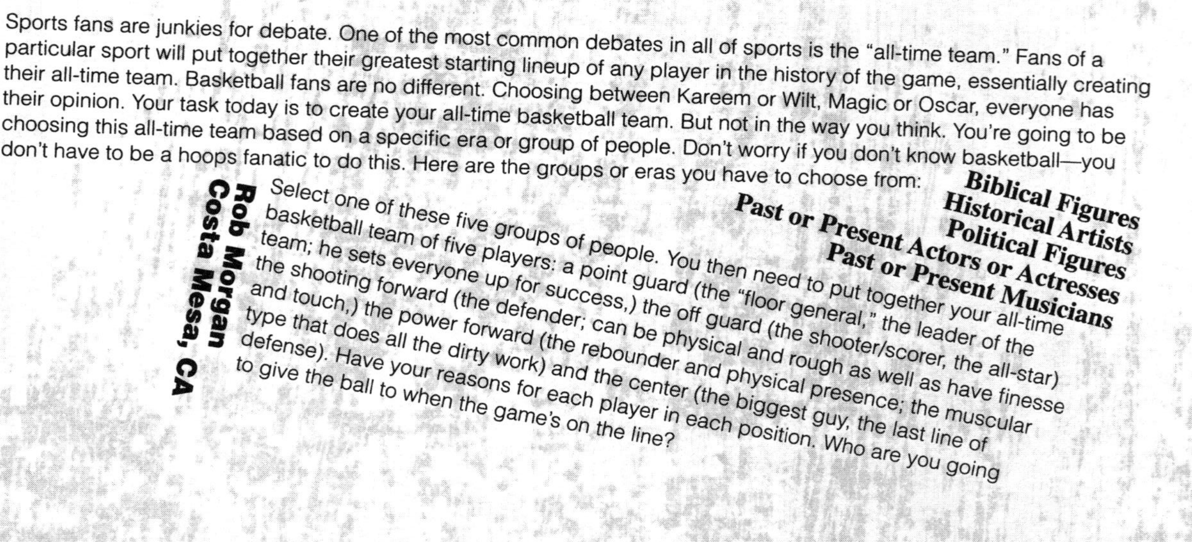

Sports fans are junkies for debate. One of the most common debates in all of sports is the "all-time team." Fans of a particular sport will put together their greatest starting lineup of any player in the history of the game, essentially creating their all-time team. Basketball fans are no different. Choosing between Kareem or Wilt, Magic or Oscar, everyone has their opinion. Your task today is to create your all-time basketball team. But not in the way you think. You're going to be choosing this all-time team based on a specific era or group of people. Don't worry if you don't know basketball—you don't have to be a hoops fanatic to do this. Here are the groups or eras you have to choose from:

Biblical Figures
Historical Artists
Political Figures
Past or Present Actors or Actresses
Past or Present Musicians

Select one of these five groups of people. You then need to put together your all-time basketball team of five players: a point guard (the "floor general," the leader of the team; he sets everyone up for success,) the off guard (the shooter/scorer, the all-star) the shooting forward (the defender; can be physical and rough as well as have finesse and touch,) the power forward (the rebounder and physical presence; the muscular type that does all the dirty work) and the center (the biggest guy, the last line of defense). Have your reasons for each player in each position. Who are you going to give the ball to when the game's on the line?

Rob Morgan
Costa Mesa, CA

Is That a Tailpipe, or Are You Just Happy To See Me?

It's a story we've heard a thousand times. An SUV walks into a party, has a little too much to drink, hooks up with an antelope, and fathers offspring. That old chestnut. It's high time you put your own spin on this age-old cautionary tale. Your task today is to choose a vehicle and an animal. These two love birds hook up and produce offspring. What would that offspring look like? What features would it take from its individual parents? He has his mother's headlights, we know.

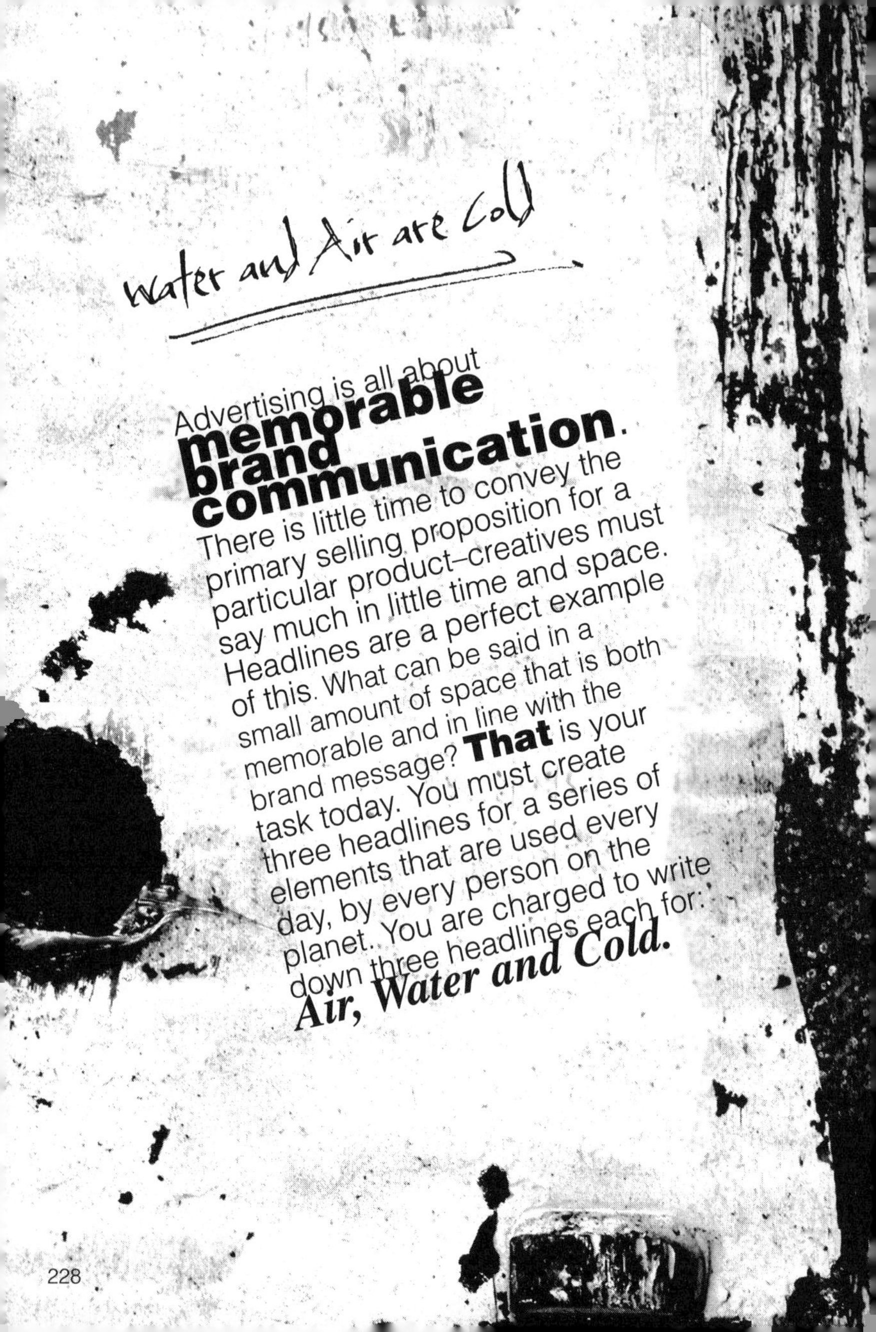
Water and Air are Cold
Advertising is all about **memorable brand communication**.
There is little time to convey the primary selling proposition for a particular product–creatives must say much in little time and space. Headlines are a perfect example of this. What can be said in a small amount of space that is both memorable and in line with the brand message? **That** is your task today. You must create three headlines for a series of elements that are used every day, by every person on the planet. You are charged to write down three headlines each for:
Air, Water and Cold.

"I'm a graphic designer for a public library, so I'm always promoting the same thing: books. ***Every verbal twist containing the word 'book' or 'read' has been done to death, and it's challenging to come up with fresh ways to promote the same 'product' year after year.*** *Trying to figure out pithy ways to promote things like 'Air' (It's a Gas!) and 'Cold' (Where Else Can You See Your Breath?) gave me a new subject to ponder. But more than that, the exercise got me to thinking about how I could make each headline as different as possible, either by wordplay, visual associations, or pointing out how the object in question relates to the viewer."*

Candace Gallant
Mount Horeb, WI

I TRIED IT!

What's Next?

We are a species of order. We cling to pattern; it's predictable and safe. We're so attracted to pattern that given certain scenarios, we can complete the scene without knowing the remaining information. For instance, 1) a man buys a lottery ticket faithfully every week for ten years, losing each time; 2) he can't get to a store to buy one this week, and on his way home he glances at a TV in a window showing the lottery numbers; and 3)...? We all know what the pattern would reveal in this scenario. Your task today is break that cycle of predictable outcomes by finishing the following scenarios in alternative ways:

1) A man walks into a bar,
2) An angry woman with a bat follows,
3)?

1) A kid gets on the bus to school one morning,
2) The door closes when he realizes there's a grizzly bear in the back of the bus,
3)?

1) A man finds an iPod on the street,
2) It has a note attached that says "play me,"
3)?

1) A woman is preparing a TV dinner one night,
2) She opens the dessert portion,
3)?

1) A man stumbles across a convenience store robbery,
2) He sees the robber about to run out of the store with a full duffle bag,
3)?

How Do I Make a Round Chimney?

Are you the type that tries to put the square peg in the round hole? Although with enough force, that equation is rather solvable either way, some things are naturally designed to be done a certain way. We're going to break that habit today. Your task today is to draw a house by only using parts of a perfect circle. You can dissect the circle any way you like, but any lines you draw must be part of a circle. You can reuse parts of the circle as many times as you like, but there should be no straight lines used. Don't forget the doorknobs—they should be easy!

Survivor: Madison Avenue

Reality TV has taken over our lives. The Home and Garden channel even has a reality TV show. What's this world coming to? If everyone and everything can have a reality TV show, then you can, too. Your task today is to create a reality TV show out of your agency, firm, studio, place of employment, whatever. Create some form of reality TV show based around your current environment. Consider how "contestants" would be selected, what they would have to do and how they would be eventually eliminated. Just leave the tiki torches out of tribal council.

Oh Say Can You Peep?

Stereotypes are one of the driving forces behind advertising, good or bad. Since stereotypes are widely known, they make easy comedy, and **comedy is often used to sell.** Stereotypes can be fun as long as they're expressed in good nature and everyone understands they are expressions of an existing stereotype and not part of our internal beliefs. We're going to let our guard down a little, laugh at ourselves a little and play with stereotypes today. Your task today is to rewrite the national anthem using one of the following musical genres as your stereotype guide:

Hip Hop
Country
Opera
Heavy Metal
Punk

Choose one of the genres above and rewrite the national anthem based on what you know about the scene, the audience, the bands/singers, etc.

Rob Morgan, Costa Mesa, CA

And Then He Said...

Go to **www.wakeupmybrain.com/cftcm/exercises/andthenhesaid.html**. Download and print the PDF document titled "storytelling." There will be five images in the document. Cut them out and turn them face-down on a table. Mix them up thoroughly, arrange them in a line, and then turn them over. You should have five images randomly aligned in a row. ***Your task is to write copy underneath each image to tell a story–sort of like a cartoon.*** *Look at the illustration in each frame, then as a whole, and create the story you will be telling.* Write dialog, scene setup, or a simple explanation of what is occurring in each of the scenes. Write no more than two sentences for each image.

What Happens From Here?

There are many aspects to great storytelling that draw the reader into the action. One of the most effective methods to grabbing the reader right from the start is creating an opening sentence that expresses a sense of intrigue. One well-known author once wrote that all stories should begin with the main character standing in the middle of a busy two-way highway. His reasoning was that the main character had to act or the story would be over. Your task today is to create ten single-sentence story openings. Don't worry about what the story that would follow would be, just create an opening sentence that would grab the reader immediately. "Once upon a time…" doesn't count.

All Aboard!

Where the lap of luxury and excitement meets the sea, you'll find a cruise ship. Cruise ships offer the finest in dining, entertainment, vacation destinations and on-board activities. As cruise ships get bigger and more expensive, developers are adding all sorts of amenities to the ship. The larger the ship, the more that can be accomplished. Your task today is to design your own fantasy cruise ship. It can be as large as you want, and can accommodate guests in whatever style or manner you'd like. This is the You Cruise Lines. Describe or sketch out the exterior of the ship, including the types of restaurants, activities and entertainment you will have on your ship. Here's to hoping it will still float when you get done with it!

Would You Like Any Fillings or Gold Caps With THAT?

The modern day drive-thru doesn't get the appreciation it deserves. It's there to keep us from having to get out of our cars and walk the twenty yards to the counter of our favorite fast food joint. It even lets us bank from our SUVs. The drive-thru is almost perfect for any application. Almost. Your task today is to list ten things that shouldn't have a drive-thru. Some things are just better left to the ambulatory masses.

Where'd You Get That Hot Chocolate, Dude?

Skiing took a back seat to snowboarding on the "cool snow sport" list years ago. With new snowboarders arriving at the slopes every day, mountain operators have built elaborate snowboard terrain for every level of boarder. It's time for the snowboard manufacturers to step up as well, with your help, of course. Your challenge today is to create the Ultimate Snowboard. This isn't just a paint job, this is high-tech marketing warfare. Create the snowboard of your dreams, something that would cater to every whim a snowboarder might have. Don't worry about whether it is aerodynamically correct. Attach and build whatever you think would be gobbled up by snowboarders. The battery pack for that onboard widescreen TV might be a bit cumbersome, but you'll figure something out!

Is That a SuperSlushee Monument Built Out of Wieners?

You wake up one morning and realize you're a Corner Quikee Mart clerk. Happens. Not only that, but your cheapskate boss has given you a task. He's a cheapskate because he doesn't allow you to throw away the unpurchased hot dogs left on the rollers at the end of the night. He wants to reuse them the next day. Naturally, no one has purchased a hot dog in weeks. Not feeling right about leaving the petrified franks on the rollers each night, you've been stashing them in the back room. Well, he found your stash. Instead of firing you, he's mandated that you "reuse" the hot dogs in a different way. He's aware of your creative background, so he's ordered you to create some other way to use the stashed hot dogs. Your only restriction is that you can't put them back on the rollers and you can't throw them away. Anything else is fair game. He'd be happy if they could help make him some money. **You'd be happy if the temp agency would call back.**

It's Good To See A Happy Potato

In the late 1940s, George Lerner created a set of plastic facial features of eyes, noses, ears and lips, with push pins for backs. These facial features were meant to be stuck to fruits and vegetables, and the first Mr. Potato Head was born. During the war, Lerner felt that parents wouldn't want to spare good fruits and vegetables for toys, so he created the plastic potato we all know and love. While Mr. Potato Head is a part of just about everyone's youth, adults are left with little to play with. Until today. It is your challenge today to create sets of eyes, ears, noses and lips. Print them out or cut them out, add push pins to the back, and find that fruit or vegetable in the refrigerator to be your very own Mr. Potato Head. The denser vegetables and fruit work better, or ones that have thick skins. Use the creations to alert unsuspecting co-workers and family members of your current mood. Mr. Frustrated Potato Head thanks you.

Go Joe!

G.I. Joe has been around since 1964, and since then, there have been many "Joes." Navy Joe, Paratrooper Joe, and others gave Joe fans more reasons to purchase more Joes. What if there were "Joes" in your world? Your task today is to identify three different "people" in your life, like family members, professions or friends. Create a "Joe" for each of them, naming them and describing their action feature. Just leave "Mother-In-Law Joe," with rolling pin action arm, out of it.

What's That Amazing Smell?

Did you know that the average human being is able to recognize approximately 10,000 different odors? That's a lot of smells! Our sense of smell is much stronger than we give it credit for. We can recall smells with a 65% accuracy rate after a whole year. ***Visual accuracy decreases 50% after just three months! Fact is...we remember smells. Your task is to remember at least twenty of them. Write down twenty things that smell great when they are cooking.***

Mmmmm.......

interview with

Jeff Fisher

In his book, ***The Savvy Designer's Guide to Success,*** Jeff quotes Pablo Picasso, saying:

"'Every child is an artist. The problem is how to remain an artist when you grow up.'

We've heard this type of statement before, in a variety of forms and translations, about getting back to a child-like view of the world. Creativity comes from an alternative view of communication, so it would make sense that we could foster a more creative mindset simply by reverting back to a child-like view of the world, where everything was new and we took everything at face value, and risk wasn't something to be avoided, but rather embraced.

'I want to play!' That Picasso quote is right on–when we were kids, everyone was an artist, and we didn't care about the quality of the work. Our art was 100% expression."

Jeff continues, "Somewhere in the process of growing up, we lost that desire to create simply for the expressive nature of it. I remember my first piece of art. **Some kid messed on my paper in class, and I turned it into a flower**. I don't remember why, I just remember doing it. I don't want to grow up. I'm a smart ass by nature, and a smart ass is constantly looking at things differently. I get paid, to a large degree, to be a smart ass, to look at stuff differently. And my mother always used to say that nothing good would come of me being a smart ass."

Logo design is one of the most challenging of all design practices, simply because the focus of the artwork is so personal to the client. It is the face of the person or business; it's called upon to actually speak to the integrity of the person or business alone. Creativity in this form of design is at a much grander scale, creativity of not only concept, but execution. ***How does he do it?*** How does he maintain THAT level of creativity on a daily basis? What activities or exercises are important to someone that is completely and wholly reliant on maintaining a creative edge? "I rarely get usable ideas while sitting in front of the computer. The computer is really just a tool. I get most of my ideas when I'm engaged in something else, in the car, in the shower. When I'm doing something more relaxing, my mind is far more open to ideas. Once a week, I have breakfast with a group of friends of mine. Retailers, marketing directors, insurance salesmen, a playwright, an actor… Anyone but a designer. It gets me out of the office and talking to a group of people that don't know design theory and who aren't already seasoned with default fonts and industry lingo.

It's considerably more inspiring to me to talk project ideas over with them and extract their differing points of view than to mull over stale image connections with colleagues. I think we get so stuck doing the work that we forget the reason we were hired to do the work… to find that different point of view."

Doesn't that* perfectly *sum up the very purpose of our industry, the quintessential reason we want to foster a more creative mindset?

Simply to find a different point of view.

Jeff Fisher Logomotives
www.jfisherlogomotives.com

I Never Knew A Pencil Sharpener Could Be So Deep

Seeing the everyday objects slightly differently is one of the keys to idea generation and creative thought. As we go through our day, we visually pass over common objects without ever really recognizing the complexity of the objects themselves. Sometimes, the best ideas are right there all the time, if we'll take the time to really examine the assets. Your task today is to take an object you look at every day and really get into it. Find something visually interesting, something with a little bit of complexity to it as an object. Not a pencil, let's say, something more interesting than that. The object should be something you look at every day but rarely see, like that stapler on your desk or the cell phone next to it. Take out some sketch paper and draw out every shape you see in that object. Turn the object over, open it up, flip it upside down, document the object in the form of shapes. These don't have to be geometric shapes, although they could, but they should be completed shapes. Don't worry about the detail within the shapes; concentrate on the shapes themselves. Even see the negative space and the shapes it produces. Draw out each shape on the paper. When you finish, look at your sheet. Isn't it amazing at what we see when we truly look at something?

It's Better Than Cleaning It!

Paint brushes are like creme-filled donuts: **Great at first, but then the aftertaste kicks in.** Clean paint brushes mean that something can get painted, which is fun, but cleaning the paint brush sucks. It takes virtually days to get it completely clean, and by then, all the fun has worn off. It's time we gave those paint brushes some other purpose. Your task today is to create ten alternative uses for the common paint brush. Not the artist kind, mind you, but the industrial "paint the house" kind of brush. Thank goodness someone invented thinner.

Is That Chest of Drawers On a Dimmer?

You use what you have, right? In everything we do, we use what we have to accomplish the goal. Sometimes it's enough, sometimes it isn't. Today, it's going to be enough. You're going to create something out of what you can see right now. Look around you.

Got it? Got a picture of everything around you? Good. You need to design a chandelier out of the things that you can see right now. Imagine what could hold the lighting, how it would hang, the balance it would need. And no, your boss does not count as "materials."

How Many Ounces of Gold Do I Need to Park Here?

You wanna park on a busy metropolitan street, it's going to cost you. And who is there to collect? The trusty parking meter. Only staying for ten minutes? No problem, you just need to deposit 209 dimes, please. Fourteen seconds late to your car? Don't fret. The ticket is only $550. Parking meters are an evil necessity. But that doesn't mean they have to be ugly or dysfunctional! Your task today is to redesign the parking meter. That may mean a different shape, that may mean a different function, it's up to you. Consider all that is distasteful about the parking meter and recreate it according to what you think would be not only helpful, but desirable to park your car along that thoroughfare. No spare change? No problem, you'll think of that!

Mmmmm... Lincoln Logs

It's inevitable. There comes a time in every toddler's life when anything that can fit in a hand MUST be able to fit in a mouth. From books to cups to pets to toys, everything is edible. While we know that most things, pets included, are certainly not meant to be lunch, there's no reason why we, as creatives, can't do something about the situation. Your challenge today is to take a toddler's toy, any toy you desire, and make it PURPOSELY edible. Consider what the pieces would be made out of, what various "flavors" might be available, and how the packaging might come into play. Be kind to the parents, too, if possible. They get cleanup duties.

That Box Is Looking At Me

Along any major city street are a variety of pale green or white junction boxes. It seems the only people who actually know what these waist-high containers are for are either city workmen, phone company employees or electricians. While they might make good stools when waiting for a bus, they aren't exactly the most beautiful of street monuments. That will change today. Your task today is to design or decorate these eyesores to make them less, well, sore. You can change the shape of the boxes, paint the boxes or even reconstruct the boxes out of some other material. **Money is no object.** Isn't that every city's motto?

When Egg Noodles Die Young

Acronyms are great ways to remember words and phrases. Since we rarely forget our own names, we rarely need to create an acronym for ourselves, but that's going to change today. Your task today is to create an acronym of your name. Take each of the letters in your first or last name and create what they stand for. For instance, if your name is "Ed," your acronym might be "Educated Driver," or "Extremely Dapper," or "Eternal Doofus." **Let's just hope your name isn't Ed. If it is, your new name today is "Arnold."** Go get 'em, Arnold.

You're a hobo.

You're not a tramp or a bum, but a hobo. Technically speaking, a hobo is one who travels to work, meaning the circumstances of their situations keep them from not only settling down in any one spot, but traveling from town to town to find meaningful temporary employment. Hobos desire to work, they just don't do it in any one spot. Hobos are resourceful, which you, as a hobo, are going to prove today. As a creative hobo, you've been hired by your current employer to do some graphic work, or write some copy, or even shoot some photography. At the end of the day, after paying you your daily wage, your employer was kind enough to allow you free reign of your environment to confiscate whatever you'd like to create your "mobile home" for the night. You spec'd out a nice place down the street at the park to rest your weary bones, and this new development has got you thinking you're going to be livin' it up tonight! Out of just the objects in your environment, design on paper your luxurious hobo living quarters.

It's like camping,

but with style!

I Call Him "Upside Down Coffee Cup Man!"

We all are familiar with the concept of action figures. Regardless of gender, toys that represent people are some of the most beloved toys of our youth. Whether those figures were from a movie or simply a well-branded character, we all played with action figures. **As adults, we don't seem to have time for action figures anymore.** Perhaps we no longer feel the need to act out scenarios and relationships. Some of us have real live action figures. They're called kids. Whatever the reason, we're going to reconcile to our action figure void today. Using only the materials you have access to in your environment, your task today is to create an action figure. The only restriction is it has to be able to stand on its own. Kung Fu grip optional.

My Guard Rail Keeps Blocking the Scanner

You just got a new client, an alternative furniture manufacturer. You questioned the meaning of "alternative furniture," and your client responded with your first project. **They have come to you with the concept of bunk desks.** *Not bunk beds, but bunk desks. They explain that they can save companies hundreds of thousands of dollars in square footage leasing by creating a desk system that takes advantage of the space above traditional offices. The idea of bunk desks would be to "stack" workers vertically, creating a desk above a desk. Your challenge today is to come up with how their theory would work. By either sketching out the idea, or describing the idea in writing, explain your proposal for the bunk desk.*

I Make A Terrible Clown

Life is more enjoyable if we learn to laugh at ourselves. And what's funnier than a clown? OK, lots of things, but we're talking about you and clowns right now. Grab a digital camera. Take a photo of yourself (not in a mirror.) Print out the photo. Now, with a pen or a set of markers, draw a clown face over yours, big nose and all. Now if anyone calls you Bozo, you can answer!

It Looks Like a Scribble

Get a blank piece of paper and a pen or pencil. Close your eyes and scribble all over the paper. Make the scribble as *random as possible* and scribble for as long or as little as you like. Open your eyes and look at what is on the paper. Now comes the fun part! ***Turn that scribble into something recognizable***. Look at the positive AND negative space. Identify the shapes within the shapes. Recognize repeating patterns. Use your imagination and **have fun!**

Derek Bender, Orlando, FL

I Knew That Xylophone Would Come in Handy One Day

We spend a lot of time at work. Whether that's "at home" at work, or at the office/studio at work, we spend many hours in our own work environment. We've seen the objects in their respective places so many times, we don't even recognize they are there anymore. Time to change that perspective and explore our environment once again. Grab a digital camera. While seated in your usual work environment, take a picture of something in your area that begins with each letter of your name. If your name is John Smith, you'll be taking nine photos, one for each letter. We're terribly sorry if your name is **Alexander Christiansen Constanstinopolis**.

I Tried It

"This exercise was quick, simple and fun. **The speed of the exercise gave me the chance for a brief creative diversion during a busy part of my day.** The simplicity of the exercise demonstrated how easily a new approach to a problem can be generated. The best part of the exercise was its entertainment value. Building each of the fourteen letters in my name was like a treasure hunt as I looked for the necessary parts and pieces."

John Kleinpeter
Irvine, CA

I Have a Full House, Marketing Directors over Production Thugs

The standard deck of cards has 52 cards. Since as far back as 1377, playing cards have used various designs, mostly geography-influenced, and have represented various denominations. Your task today is to put playing cards not only in the 21st century, but right in your own back yard. You're going to redesign the standard deck of cards to represent either your current place of employment or your family. First, you'll need to create the four "suits." Your only restriction is you can't use spades, clubs, diamonds or hearts. Next, you'll need to create the face cards: jacks, queens and kings. Finally, you'll need to create the ace. When you're done, consider printing up your cards and playing a little. The joker is up to you!

Sure Beats Hand Puppets

Everyone can make a hand shadow. Put your hands in between a beam of light and something solid, hook your thumbs and wave your hands and you have the shadow of a bird. Some folks can make just about anything appear in the shadow, from barking dogs to boxers duking it out. While most of us would pull a tendon trying something unusual, there is a way we can create a pretty cool shadow effect. Your task today is to create a light stencil. Identify a small, reachable light source, like a desk lamp or track lighting.

Measure the diameter of the shade housing of the light. Most common track lighting cans are roughly 4-6 inches in diameter. Draw out the diameter you just measured plus an extra two inches on a piece of paper. This is your workspace.

Now, create some form of design, like your logo or perhaps download a jack-o-lantern template from one of many template websites. Within the circle you created, draw out the design, then either using an X-Acto blade or scissors, cut out the design only. Wrap the design so it is centered over the housing of the light, securing it with a rubber band or piece of tape. Turn the light so it is facing a solid surface, turn it on, and see what appears. Grab a digital camera and take a picture of your shadow design. Be sure to remove the template from the light after you've taken a picture. Remember, lights are hot and paper is flammable!

Fire In The Hole!

The plastic spoon is quietly one of the greatest inventions known to man. What would we eat plastic shot cups of processed chocolate pudding with, if it weren't for our pint-sized friend? And stirring? Don't even think about it. But there is one usage category that the plastic spoon is slow to take leadership of, and that's the flinging category. Little-known fact about plastic spoons: They make GREAT flingers, of just about any semi-weighted material! It's time to test it out. You're going to need a friend or two for this contest. It's a Flinging Contest. Distance wins. Materials are up to you. Find the material that you think the plastic spoon will best fling for distance and have a fling-off. (Try to aim away from the boss' door.)

Doesn't Anyone Wear Yellow Anymore?

What child doesn't love to color? Crayons are the beginning of a life filled with color and art. Since 1903, when the first box of eight color crayons was sold, those eight colors have paved the way to some of the most fun we've ever had introducing color into our worlds. Today, we're going to revisit those eight colors. Grab a digital camera. Your task today is to take a picture of something that is one of the eight colors in the standard box of crayons. You should be taking eight pictures, one each of something that represents blue, red, yellow, orange, green, purple, brown and black. The picture should be framed in such a way that the color in question is completely dominant, it should take up most of the frame. There should be no question what color the picture is for. Thank you, Crayola!

It's Up, And It's Good!

Sometimes, you're just in the mood to kick a football through the uprights. Happens to everyone. Who are we to stop you? But before you have Lucy in the office next to you hold the football in the hall, how about considering a slightly less violent way to satisfy your pigskin cravings. Let's start with a paper football. Take a standard piece of notebook paper out, tear it in half long way (so you have a 4.25 x 11 piece), then fold it in half the same way (now it's a little over 2 x 11). Then, start folding the paper vertically in a triangle, like you would a flag. Start at the bottom and work your way up until all you have is a triangle. Tape the remaining flap down. Now that you have your football, all you need is the field goal. Stand two vertical objects up about ten feet away, and about ten inches apart from one another. There's the goal post. Find a flat surface, and hold your football down with one finger on the tip, the other tip on the flat surface and the third point towards you. It should be standing on end, held only by your finger. Use your other hand to put your thumb and fore finger together and "flick" the football towards the goal. Flicking it on the lower half and aiming slightly upwards will help get it airborne. Get it to cross through the uprights. **Score!**

Haiku-A-Gogo!

What in the haiku is a "haiku?"

Simply put, haiku is a form of poetry. While there are many styles and forms of haiku, one of the most popular iterations is a poem that is three lines, and follows this formula:

5 syllables
7 syllables
5 syllables

The 5-7-5 form is the only restriction, the poem doesn't have to rhyme. Your task today is to write a haiku about one of the following subjects:

Your typical day
Your boss
Grape jelly
Country music
The eraser
Garbage
Cheese

Creatures of Habit

Humans love repetition. We go to the same places, eat the same things, sleep on the same side of the bed and watch the same shows night after night. **We love repetition because we find comfort in it.** Every one of us has a routine. Even if we don't know it, we have certain tasks that we perform the same way every day. **Routine can often be a deterrent to creativity.** In routine, we miss experiencing something in a new way, and the lack of this experience may effect what we can bring to the table during idea generation. Before we can assess our routine, we have to be aware of it. Grab a digital camera. Take fifteen photos of things that you do everyday, things that are part of your routine. Take nothing for granted, think about every thing you do and in what order. Even think abut how you perform those individual tasks. After documenting this, try to change one routine every day. Even the slightest change in perspective can have unexpected results.

If You Want To See Your Beloved Pencil Sharpener Alive...

You're a mastermind criminal. Who isn't? But you know something almost every other criminal doesn't know: **Practice makes perfect.** Your task today is to practice the devious skill of thievery. First, you must plan. You're going to "borrow" something from someone's office or desk. You may have to go scope it out, find the right person and the right object. Find someone that will be willing to play along when the practice begins. Got it? Good. Now, you're going to replace the object you "borrow" with a riddle alerting the victim that something was "borrowed" and if they want it back, they have to solve the riddle. Once you know which object you will be "borrowing," create the riddle and type it out or cut out the words from a magazine. So they won't guess your handwriting, of course! Then, in your stealthiest mode, "borrow" the object and leave the note. If you really think you're a mastermind criminal and expert actor, even play dumb and find the note for them, or try and help them solve it when they find it. Now, go back to your desk, rub your hands together and bellow out your most maniacal evil laugh.

Mooohohohohoho haaahahahaha!

A Buffalo Would Definitely Destroy An Eagle In A Fight

A buffalo would definitely destroy an eagle in a fight. Is there a greater sports event in North America than the NCAA Division I Men's Basketball Tournament? OK, that may be up for debate, but what isn't debatable is the popularity of the office pool. From rabid college basketball fans to the unknowing, uncaring office manager, anyone can fill out the 64 team brackets. Many people have unusual methods for picking the winners of each game. From choosing which team's mascot would win in a bar fight to which team is farther west on the map, everyone has a theory. Even if you know nothing about the tournament, you can create the top five most inventive ways to pick the winners of 32 college basketball games. Your task today is to do just that. Choose and survive!

Is That For a Dog Food Company?

Identity design is one of the most challenging mediums to work in. The communication of the nature of someone's business is a very personal type of design. Many times, the logo mark doesn't accurately communicate the type of business the mark is meant to express. **Let's explore that void a little today.** You'll need an additional willing participant for this exercise. Each of you grab a separate magazine that can be cut up, and keep which magazine you are using a secret. As each of you go through your magazine, cut out logos you find without the name of the company attached, just the mark itself. As you do this, write down what company and industry the mark is for. Try to find between five and ten examples. When you have completed this, either paste the marks up on a piece of paper or lay them out on a desk. Have your counterpart attempt to define the industry or company associated with each mark. Then you do the same with the marks he/she cut out. Notice how good design communicates a great deal about the company. As creatives, we should strive to communicate in the most effective ways in each opportunity we are given.

interview with

Sayles Graphic Design

John Sayles and ***Sheree Clark*** founded Sayles Graphic Design in 1985 with a unique concept they call Art/Smart. John, a creative, driven artist, leads his department doing what they do best: designing. Although Sheree offers creative input, her team's focus is client service and business operations. Worlds apart in titles, the two find common ground when idea generation is at a premium. "Ever since I have known her," John begins, "Sheree has said she is not a creative person visually. The fact is, however, she has some very unique ideas and I give her credit for having a wonderful design eye. The whole staff at Sayles Graphic Design participates in weekly staff meetings and we all brainstorm for ideas. Sheree gives me and the other designers honest and constructive feedback."

A visit to the portfolio section of the studio's web site will definitely reinforce a group approach to idea generation and brainstorming. The visual variety is creatively vast and decisively on target. Getting to and maintaining that level of creative output can be an arduous task, but John and Sheree have the right approach to creative management. "I am always telling my staff 'design is all around you'," John says, "I believe that if you are awake, you are in a position to learn and enhance your creativity."

Sheree, John, and Tikee

"I don't orchestrate other peoples' creative growth, but that doesn't mean I don't encourage it. *I just don't plan events or try to force people on my staff do the same things that I do.* I think we each need to find our own way. The creative journey is a highly personal one. One thing we do here to help give a 'break in the action' is to have some fun times together as a staff. We own our building and there is a built-in grill outside. On **birthdays**—and most Fridays during the summer—we grill out and maybe have a pot luck. We also have surprise breakfasts every now and then when Sheree and I 'kidnap' the group and go have breakfast somewhere."

Sheree adds "Oh, there are tons of things we do to keep the team fresh. Some stuff is small and silly—like when we give door prizes out at staff meetings and such. By shaking up what would ordinarily be a mundane event, you can ***breathe new creative life into an organization.***

When I facilitate a day-long meeting, I nearly always give the group an assignment to complete ahead of time; something that requires introspection and thoughts outside of the norm. For example, I recently gave each member of a design firm I work with the task of doing something—by themselves—that made them feel uncomfortable. One person attended a religious revival and another jumped out of an airplane!"

Sheree has a special passion for keeping people creative. "In addition to being a partner at Sayles Graphic Design, I am a consultant to creative organizations and businesses. I often invent exercises for teams when I facilitate sessions, and usually the exercises are meant to help the group get 'unstuck' or to help them loosen up. The best way I know to enhance the level of creative output from a group is to get the participants to relax. I do that by helping to create an atmosphere of trust and acceptance. I am also big on doing post mortems–looking at a project after the dust has settled in order to evaluate the process and the outcome. I think it is important to future efforts to learn from success—and failures—of the past."

It's clear that Sayles Graphic Design is in for far more success than failure.

Sayles Graphic Design
www.saylesdesign.com

HEY! She Has My Hairdo!

Trends are inevitable. Whther it's fashion, music, food, color, font, layout or hairstyle, trends create tendencies that are adopted by the masses. Today, we're going to work on identifying trends, both in style and design. Grab any magazine that is handy. Flip through the magazine and identify at least fifteen trends you see. They can be *style-oriented*, like fashion, or they can be design-oriented, like font choices. Put Post-it notes on each instance you find and write the trend on the Post-it note. As we improve our ability to recognize trends, we can begin to understand how trends make their way into our creative thoughts. **Are the ideas we are generating truly creative and unique, or are they expressions of current trends?**

Dude, Feel Free To Pop a Mint

Got your digital camera ready? Good. You might need a medical mask as well. Your task today is to capture the dreaded causes of halitosis, commonly known as… **bad breath!**

Take your camera around and take pictures of at least twenty things that cause bad breath.

Is It a Star?

Symbols and graphic depictions have been around since man first picked up a piece of burnt wood and started drawing on the wall to explain events and communicate ideas to his fellow cave-dwellers. Since then, certain symbols have become so engrained in society that it is difficult to display them as anything else while still effectively communicating your message.

The task therefore is to ***create new recognizable symbols for:***

a) a sun
b) a star
c) a moon
d) a man

Consider how these elements are associated, what they produce or even what we've learned about these items since the time of cave drawings.

Marc Swarbrick, Nottinghamshire, England

Mini-It!

Size is a wonderful differentiator. Without size, how would we describe the relationship between two things? The tall guy, the **thick** steak, the jumbo size… they all refer to the size of the subject. Grab a digital camera. Your challenge today is to take ten photos of things that have to do with relative size. They should be either the epitome of or a descriptor of size, as it relates to another object. For instance, a medium soft drink cup. The "medium" infers that there is a smaller size and a larger size out there somewhere. Find ten things (other than a soft drink cup!) that infer size.

How Do You Sell "And?"

Take any book off of a nearby shelf. Open to a page randomly. **Choose five words that pop off the page at you** and write them down on a piece of paper. Now, look around the room and pick the first object that jumps out at you. That object will now be your "product" for this exercise. Take your five words and create five headlines—using each of these words—for an ad to sell that product.

Alexandra Sokol, Los Angeles, CA

I TRIED IT

"This was a tough excercise because of the difficult words I chose. However, it trains the mind to come up with different locations, situations, users, tasks, etc. A real eye-opener for me on how to approach copywriting!"

Tjerja Geerts,
Amstelveen, The Netherlands

I Changed That... I Think

Change is good. Change brings newness and the air of unknown experience. Change is fresh. But alas, change is difficult. We find comfort in unchange. Unchange is familiar and expected and known. Not all things need to change, but introducing some change into our lives is healthy. Grab a digital camera. Your task today is to take ten photos of things that need to be changed. These don't have to be life-altering things; they can be small, like the batteries in a flashlight; or big, like a career. Find ten things that need to be changed and capture them. If one of yours is a baby, go ahead and do that. Soon. Please.

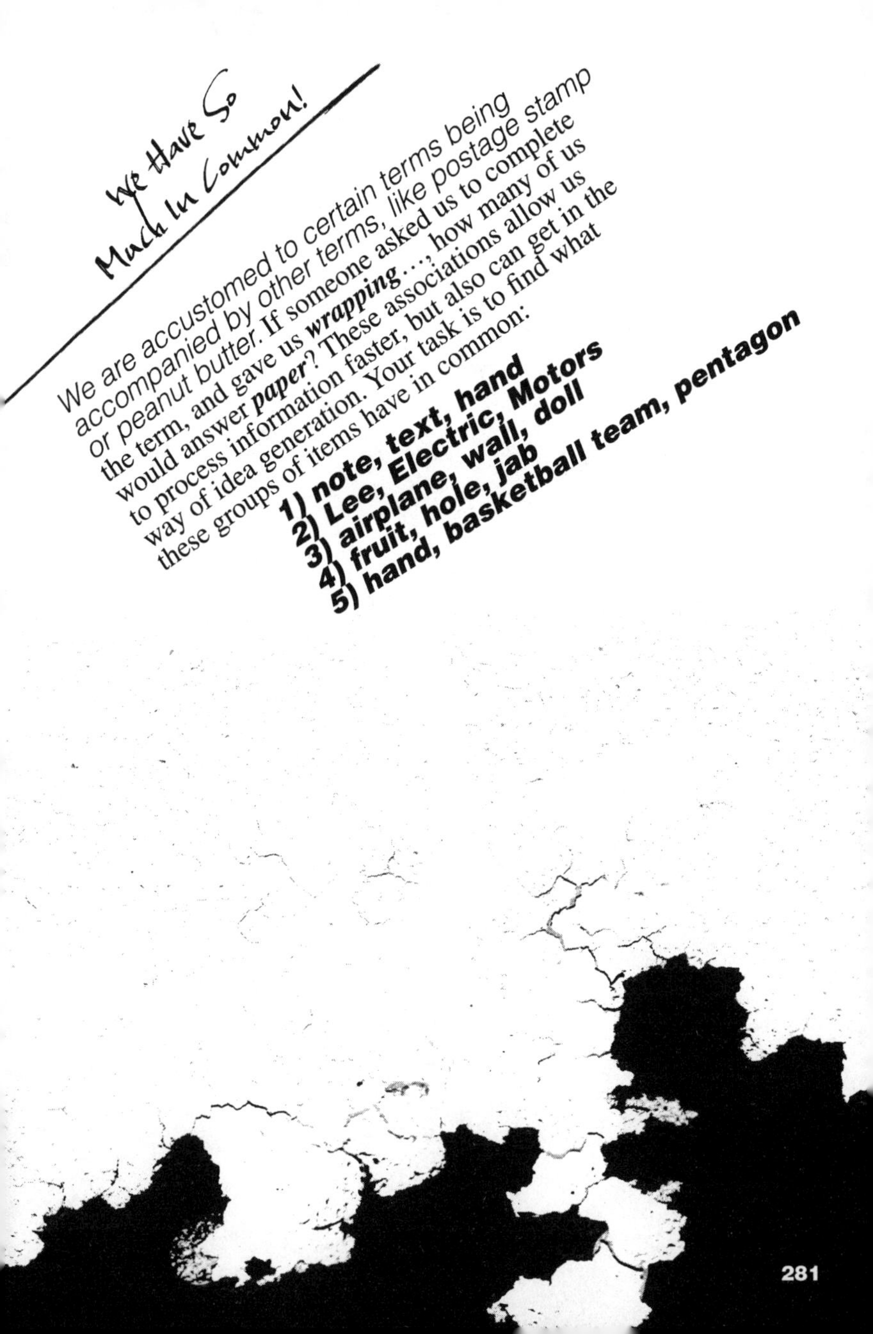

We Have So Much In Common!

We are accustomed to certain terms being accompanied by other terms, like postage stamp or peanut butter. If someone asked us to complete the term, and gave us ***wrapping***…, how many of us would answer ***paper***? These associations allow us to process information faster, but also can get in the way of idea generation. Your task is to find what these groups of items have in common:

1) note, text, hand
2) Lee, Electric, Motors
3) airplane, wall, doll
4) fruit, hole, jab
5) hand, basketball team, pentagon

I Knew I Should Have Saved That Copy of Ice Fishing Illustrated

How many times have you thumbed through a magazine, put it down, and immediately forgotten ninety-five percent of what you just experienced? As a culture, we have little time to take in everything we experience in a publication. ***As creatives, we benefit from the ability to experience as much input as we can,*** even taking notice of the subtleties within the overload of information most magazines provide. Your task today is to explore this discipline a little more. Grab a magazine that can be cut up, and a pair of scissors. As you thumb through the magazine, cut out any image and word you come across that satisfies the following statement: "That's not going to end well."

If you're feeling spicy, paste the cut-outs to paper and put them in a binder. Write the phrase on a cover sheet and put it at the beginning. Consider creating phrases for projects you are working on and do the same thing to that phrase. You might be surprised at what inspiration appears!

Does This Color Go With My Work Boots?

Men. **Manly** men. Manly men don't carry un-manly men things. It's not manly. Manly men don't coordinate clothing and accessories, they don't order caesar salads and they don't carry umbrellas. Umbrellas are NOT manly. Manly men say they don't mind getting wet, it's just water. The truth is, and don't tell anyone, but manly men actually do mind getting wet. It makes them cold. Manly men say they don't mind being cold, but they do. If only they could carry and use an umbrella without giving up any manliness. The trick would be that the umbrella would have to be cool. **And manly.** That is your challenge today. Re-engineer the common umbrella to make it acceptable for a manly man to use it. It'll need more than a paint job, it'll need some thought as to what can be created to make the umbrella manly again. The only restriction is that, at its very core, it has to keep rain off the manly man. His tootsies might get wrinkled, and no manly man wants that.

How Do You Get Your Lips Way Up There?

Laughter is the best medicine. And what's funnier than people you know and love making the funniest faces possible? **Nothing, that's what.** Grab a digital camera. Your task today is simple: Find ten people around you right now and get them to make the funniest face they have while you snap their picture. Feel free to use these pictures as blackmail later.

Big Brother is not only watching, He's Brewing Cups of Coffee for You!

Satellites are cool. They give us cell phones, commercial-free radio, and on-demand movies. They track our weather, our cars, and our world leaders! GPS systems can even e-mail us when our windshield wiper fluid is low! With the increased advancements in satellite services and GPS tracking, there's got to be a host of convenient, everyday uses. Your task today is to come up with at least ten everyday, time-saving and helpful uses for GPS/satellite navigation in your life. If they can unlock our doors for us when our keys are inside, what else can they do?

How About Dessert?

If you're not familiar with what a "table tent" is, you're not alone. Although the term may not be familiar, the item surely is. Simply put, a table tent is the three-sided, triangular, cardboard pop-up advertisement found on restaurant tables all over the world. The concept of the table tent has lured countless thousands of people to order everything from seasoned fries to gift certificates. These effective little structures are both noticeable and clumsy. They often are intrusive to the meal, more than occasionally finding their way onto a neighboring table. It's time you came up with a better idea. Either sketch out or write out a better idea for table-side advertising. It can be printed, electronic–whatever you like–and it can exist anywhere around or on the table.

I TRIED IT

"One of my hobbies is wood carving, and doing this exercise strangely reminded me of the process I do when starting a new carving project. You would think they would be completely different, but somehow, this exercise took that same creative path.

One of the best pieces of advice I ever got was from this older gentleman who told me *'the hardest part of a thousand mile journey is the first step.'* Sometimes before I start to do a carving, I'll just sit and look at that piece of wood for a long time. I've even gotten up and left because I couldn't make that first cut. The fear of the length of the journey keeps me from ever starting. But once I start, and if I keep taking steps along the journey, I find that my mind wanders away from the road and onto the scenery, and it's in the scenery we find the joy of the journey.

That's what happens when I start a carving. If I can just get myself to start creating and stop worrying about how far away I am from finishing, I find the places my mind goes to be far more creative than I ever thought. That's how the process went with the table tent.

My first thought was just to have a picture under a dish, and as you eat your meal the picture starts to appear. But why not take it a step further? Why not take it a thousand steps further? I like to let my mind go into the craziest of places. The fact that I simply began the process led me to some ideas that are far-fetched, fairly impractical, but insanely fun!

Guess the creative process really isn't that different from medium to medium after all!"

Mike Pierce, Los Alamitos, CA

Is that Hairnet Real?

Magnificent memorials are deservedly erected to honor those in military service, or those who have done great deeds, but **what about the everyday hero?** What sort of monument should the guy that feeds the sharks at the local marine amusement park receive? Or the gas station attendant that quickly and happily provided directions to your lost weekend? It's high time the everyday hero got his due. Your task is to create a memorial for these three everyday heroes:

1) Elementary School Bus Driver
2) Hotel Housekeeping
3) High School Cafeteria Worker

Denise Weyhrich, Orange, CA

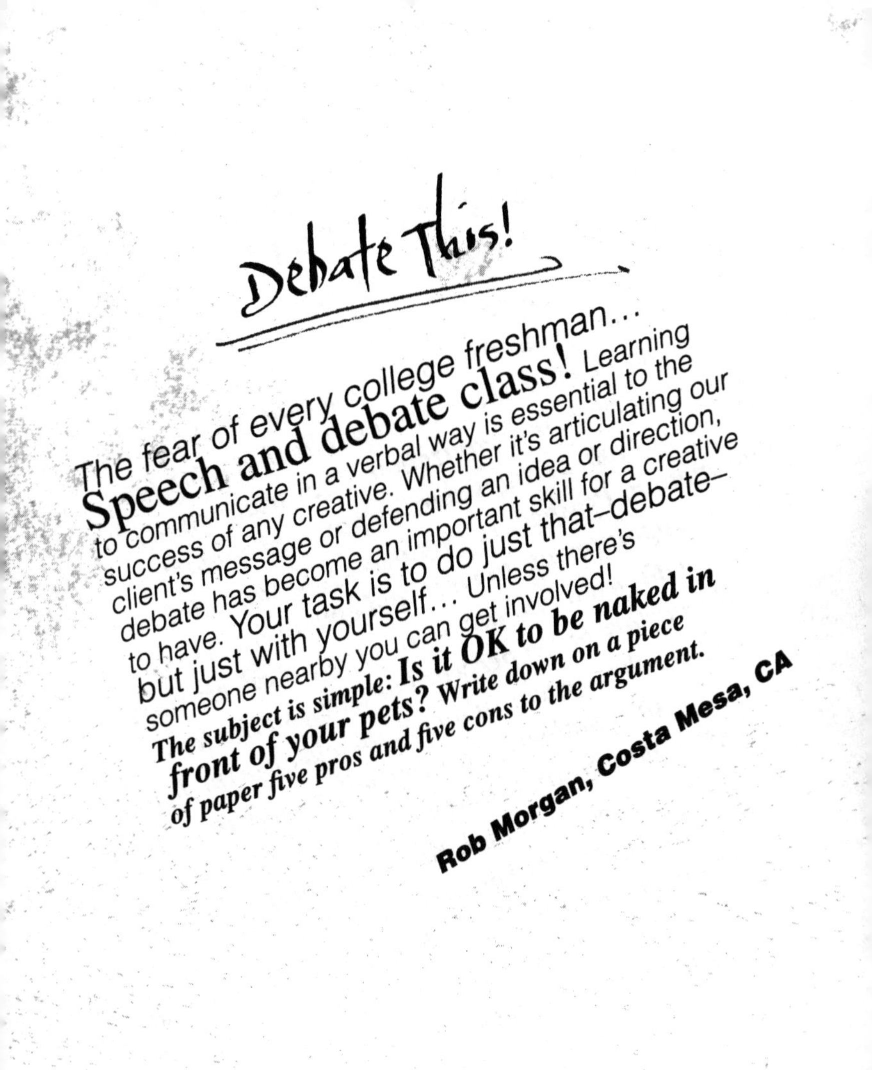

Debate This!

The fear of every college freshman… **Speech and debate class!** Learning to communicate in a verbal way is essential to the success of any creative. Whether it's articulating our client's message or defending an idea or direction, debate has become an important skill for a creative to have. Your task is to do just that–debate–but just with yourself… Unless there's someone nearby you can get involved!

The subject is simple: Is it OK to be naked in front of your pets? Write down on a piece of paper five pros and five cons to the argument.

Rob Morgan, Costa Mesa, CA

EXTRA, EXTRA! READ ALL ABOUT IT!

For years, the want ads have been a resource for those seeking employment. Employers place ads in the local newspaper alerting the general public that a job has opened up in their organization. They traditionally list the type of job, perhaps starting pay, and contact information. Prospective employees find said ads and set up appointments to meet said employers. As is the case with just about any word-oriented advertising, the ads are billed per word or letter, so the fewer letters that appear in an ad, the cheaper the listing is for the employer. This has led to some interesting hyphenations and short-order language that we have all come to understand. Your task today is to bond with the language and abbreviations of the want ad and create an ad of no more than fifty letters for your job. Inform prospective employees of exactly what to expect while selling your position to the best of your ability. (This isn't a foreshadowing or anything, we promise.)

Is That a Paisley Screensaver?

We don't notice it, but we are surrounded with patterns. Patterns are safe, patterns give us order, and we like order. Visual patterns, audible patterns, even touchable patterns. Your task today is to spend a couple minutes locating patterns. Grab a digital camera and take twenty-five photos of things in a pattern.

The Wright Bros. Would Be Proud!

Who doesn't like paper airplanes? You're going to need at least one other willing contestant for this contest. Simple task: **create a paper airplane that will fly the farthest.** It doesn't have to be the prettiest or the coolest, just fly the farthest. This will work best if you have at least a second-story window to throw it from, but if not, just find an area either inside or outside to launch from. Consider building materials, add-ons or take-aways, and trajectory. **Now go kick someone's butt!**

Balder-what?

It's likely we've all played the word game Balderdash, the game where you make up a definition to a strange but real word, and you try to get people to vote for your bogus definition. **We're going to play a little Balderdash right now,** only these words can't be found in a dictionary. Your task is to come up with your own definitions for these ten words:

1. Izzard
2. Voise
3. Visamush
4. Cubular
5. Limacious
6. Wimple
7. Zazz
8. Hottage
9. Irratainment
10. Screenpeep

Lauren Goldberg, Chicago, IL

interview with JOHN FOSTER

vice president, fuszion collaborative

Among the bevy of studio names are firms that describe themselves as "agency," "creative," "design," and even "yard." ***But what does it mean when you describe yourself as a "collaborative?"*** That's the case with Fuszion Collaborative, and vice president John Foster. Illustration led John to design, and design has led him to a passionate pursuit of creativity. "Creativity is the intangible," John says. ***"Design is visual problem solving*** and the creative solution is what separates it from the marvels of engineering or reconstructing a race car engine. You can grow it and feed it and watch it evolve as you age and experience different things. The beautiful thing is that it is different for everyone. Engineers will be striving for the same result in solving a problem in much the same manner–whereas designers will strive for the same result (or level of success) but ***they will all take very different routes to the final solution."***

With a name like Fuszion and a group defined as a Collaborative, creativity is obviously a collective pursuit. "We have a flat management style, and everyone from the principal to the intern knows not only that they can contribute to the creative conversation on any project in the studio but also that they are **EXPECTED** to contribute. This has made for the wonderful situation where some days I can be the best designer in the office and others where I can be the worst, as we all challenge one another constantly."

"As far as the collaborative nature of this environment, you know, we go bowling, *we brainstorm constantly*, we encourage research outside of the studio. We share our life experiences and tap them for inspiration, but we are also very busy at all times because we push each project until we have to present it to the client. We place a premium on creative thinking above all else, so our designers have displayed that ability before they arrive here. What we truly do is foster a creative environment where the expectations for the work are high, and that operates as the driving force."

John is clearly a gifted illustrator and designer, and although those mediums have decisively different processes, ***the pursuit of creative solutions remains the same***. "It's funny," John says, "when I started in the business, the majority of my creativity spilled out in my illustration work as I struggled with design. As I gained experience, the desire to make the most of my design work was a driving force. I think that's an important aspect to increasing the quality of your work: the desire to do the best possible job regardless of what project you are working on. If left with only a two-color newsletter to work on, then it's important to produce the most amazing newsletter anyone has ever seen. ***I also used my illustration skills to create original art regardless of budget or time constraints.*** This allowed me to stretch my creative muscles in a medium I loved, regardless of what jobs I was working on. As the scale of my projects grew and I moved into a management/creative position, I now push the creative boundaries of whatever I am working on, whether it is design-related or business-related." John is also an author, penning design books that inspire and encourage idea generation and creative thought. "As for the writing, I just do what comes naturally and trust an editor to catch me if I've sped off in the wrong direction. ***I have developed an incredibly thick skin when it comes to design***, a relatively thick skin in regards to illustration, and I am a blubbering nine-year-old girl inside when it comes to criticism of my writing."

He blubbers little these days, that's for certain!

Fuszion Collaborative
www.fuszion.com

Hi, I'm Fido

Our pets have claimed permanent residence on our love chart. Many people give their pets child-like attention, going so far as to dress them up in kids' clothes and pampering them with gifts. Likewise, naming our pets has become just as nerve-racking as naming our children. It has to be the perfect name, one that describes that pet perfectly, whether it be by color, size, disposition or attitude. We name our pets with care. But what if our pets were given the task of naming us? What would our pet names be? That's your task. ***Write down ten names that your pet would give to you.*** If you have a willing friend to work with, write down their ten pet names as they write down your ten pet names. Then compare!

Cool Vanishing Point!

Proper perspective is a learned skill for artists. Creating scenes where the perspective is off will immediately cause the viewer discomfort. **Recognizing perspective is the first step to developing the skill to create it when needed.** Perspective is most recognized when the view of the person is in a place to recognize distance, like standing in the middle of a railroad track and seeing the tracks come together in the distance, or standing at the base of a wall and seeing the lines of the wall get closer the farther away they travel. Grab a digital camera. Take ten photos of things in perspective. You might have to take a few shots of objects at very close range or at odd angles to create the desired shot. Start by standing at the start of a wall and taking a shot of the wall as it goes away. That's one!

One Meeelyun Daaaaahhllers!

Comic book villains are pretty predictable characters. ***They all are physically warped in some way. They all have an evil plan, have an evil laugh, catch the good guy, set some escapable doom for the good guy only to leave before finishing the hero off, then they all escape at the end to do it all over again next week.*** Mike Myers made an exaggeration of this character when he portrayed Dr. Evil in the Austin Powers series. We all have a little Dr. Evil in us. Today, you're going to let him out. Today, you're going to create your own over-the-top comic book villain. Describe his/her physical features (and how he/she got that way), what group or organization wronged him/her, what evil plan he/she has cooked up, his/her weapons, the secret location of his/her evil lair and his/her demands. Create the doomsday machine he/she builds for the hero.

Mooooohoo hooohaha!

I'm Flippin' SWEET!

Animation is a simple concept. You take an image, create a still shot of that image, move the image slightly, take another shot, move the image again, and so on and so on. The simplest form of animation is the flip book animation. In flip book animation, you draw a character or scene on one page of a multi-page book, then lift up that page and draw the character movement on the next page, lift that page and draw the character movements again, each time creating slight movements to create animation cells. Then, when you're all done, you flip through the pages with your thumb to see the character move by flipping through the pages quickly. Your task today is to create a flip book animation in the corner of your sketchbook. If you don't have a sketchbook, gather some paper together, cut the pages in half, then half again and stack them up. Use as many sheets as you deem necessary to complete your animation. When you get all done, you can even use your camera phone's video function to record it, and now you're an animator! **Watch out, Pixar!**

Retreat! Retreat!

There was not much more exciting than when we were kids and we found clean, empty cardboard boxes, had access to scissors and tape, and plenty of lazy summer days. Making forts is a rite of passage. We'd get a couple good-sized boxes and we could create a fortress that would protect us from the greatest of perilous invaders. ***Now that we're adults, we're far too busy for such tomfoolery.*** We don't have the time, nor do we care about those clean, empty boxes over there. Even if we have a closet full of arts and crafts tools. Who cares that the boss is gone for the rest of the day and that the project we're working on is stalled until a client returns. We're far too grown up to make a fort, aren't we? Childish activity, and a complete waste of time. Huh? What's that? Did you just say that if we were kids and we weren't so grown up, that you could build a way cooler fort than me? You didn't just say that, did you? **Oh, you're toast!** Your task today is to imagine you have six boxes, each 42" x 42" x 42". You have four thick, sturdy cardboard dowels, 12" long and 4" in circumference. You have an office supply closet full of, well, office supplies. And you have your natural desire to build the sweetest fort ever designed. You can take the boxes apart, keep them together, attach them as you see fit, whatever you want. Just make sure you answer the phones. It might be the boss coming back!

I Don't Think They Make a Slushee That Big

Idea generation is most effective when we get our ideas out of our head, document them in some form, then empty our heads to make room for new ideas. This tends to be more difficult than it sounds, as most of us put values on our ideas, meaning we believe certain ideas are "better" than others, and we have a hard time letting go of those for others we feel are simply second best. The truth is, maybe those first ideas are the best ideas, but you'll never know if you don't spend time generating others to compare them to. The good thing is that you can practice idea generation; it's a skill that can be learned. Today's task is to work on idea generation. Come up with 25 ways to use a common cardboard dowel, like the cardboard cylinder that is left when the paper towels are all gone. (Holding up paper towels is NOT one of them!)

I TRIED IT

"As an independent designer, I don't have other creative professionals around to brainstorm with or to turn to for inspiration. I found these exercises to be a great way for me to get away from my daily routine and get my creative juices flowing again, by forcing me to look at and see things differently. **After completing this exercise, I was able to finish my article easily (as my writer's block was gone), and found new inspiration in even my most routine projects."**

Tamar Wallace,
Boston, MA

Tag, You're It!

Everyone is familiar with a stapler. They've been a staple (pun intended) of our office culture for years. We've all seen staplers, used staplers and are well versed in their purpose. You now have five minutes to come up with ten unconventional ways to use a stapler. And it can't be to staple something. Look at it closely, open it up, recognize the shapes it makes. Turn it upside down, lay it on its side. Come up with ten ways to use a stapler for a purpose other than its intended calling.

Callene Abernathy, Port Orchard, WA

Did That Guy Just Say "Shucks?"

Ever sit at a coffeeshop or diner and see two people having a conversation across the room, and wonder what they were saying? She's very animated and visibly upset, but he's defensive and scolded. We start putting words in their mouths, imagining what the situation is and what they are saying. Today, we're going to put words into a few people's mouth. Go to www.wakeupmybrain.com/cftcm/exercises/talkbubbles.pdf. Print out each of the five pages. In the talk bubbles, write what you think the conversation is. If you're feeling saucy, and you have someone who is willing to participate with you, write one of the bubbles and have your partner write the other.

Wanna Play Some Mini Desk Volleyball?

There are hundreds of popular desk novelties available for that activity-minded executive. From bonzai trees and zen gardens to miniature billiards tables and putting greens. Each miniature desk activity comes with its own equipment, layout and unique characteristics. Your task today is to create your own miniature desk activity. Create what it looks like, the equipment and the purpose. Consider its size and placement on the desk. It may even have an alternative purpose, like how a cell phone also has a camera. Now if it could only come with miniature drinks and a miniature DJ, we'll be set!

Have You Ever Noticed That Before?

As we get accustomed to certain visuals, we often overlook many aspects of their character. Our usual work spaces are no different. *We're going to spend a few moments reacquainting ourselves with the character of our spaces. With a digital camera take five pictures each of the following criteria:*

Things that are brown
Things that are made of wood
Things that are cold to the touch
Things that make noise
Things that have moveable parts

If you don't have a digital camera, write them on a piece of paper.

Desks Ahoy!

Although you already have a contingency plan for this very scenario, it's time you rethink it. As is often the case where you live, the dam has completely given way, and a wall of water is headed your way right this very second. You only have time to build a boat for yourself, and you only have time to build it out of the things you can see right now from your chair. look around you and begin to identify what you're going to use to build a floatation device when the wave hits. You can only use the materials you can see right now to build the deck of the boat, bind pieces together, create a rudder or oars or even a sail. It has to be strong enough to hold you and perhaps something you bring with you to live on for the time you're afloat, like your laptop or iPod of course!

For Sale

Want ads are a staple of newspaper advertising. While want ads often describe an item, the reality of how want ads are sold (by the letter) creates an environment where most inconsequential information about the product or service is left out. Your task today is to find a want ad, either in a physical newspaper or online newspaper website, and to create a story that describes the history of the item being sold, the story of that object, the owner and why it's being sold. The farther "out there" the story is, the better. Anyone can sell speakers that fell off the back of a truck!

Pablo is Calling!

Open your desk drawer, purse, briefcase or other clutter-filled area. Pull three items out randomly. Take a sheet of paper and place the items on the paper in some random composition. They can overlap if you wish. Now trace around the items. Put the items away. ***Now fill in or flesh out the outlines by turning them into other "things."*** See if you can create a connected picture with them. And no, it doesn't need to be a Picasso (though it might look like one!)

Misha Mace, Bellingham, WA

I Can't Hear You, I'm Screaming

The ***exclamation point*** is the aerobics instructor of punctuation marks. It means so many things, and they're all relatively loud. Ending important sentences for years now, the ***exclamation point*** can mean you are supposed to read that last sentence in the spirit of anger, fear, excitement, joy or happiness. Or it can simply imply that you should read it louder than other sentences. It's hard to know exactly what it means without the context of the sentence. Until today. Your challenge today is to create "degrees" of ***exclamation points***. You are to create new punctuation to replace the ***exclamation point*** that better describes the following exclamations:

Anger
Happiness
Excitement
Fear
Loud

You can use the ***exclamation point*** as a design element, or you can create your own brand new punctuation. Alright!!!

How Could I Live Without My Combination Hot Dog Cooker and Bun Warmer?

We have been witness to some great inventions. For those of us who remember life without the microwave, we have no idea how we got along without it. For every ten average items we see enter the marketplace, there is one that stands out as an amazing, how-could-I-ever-have-survived-without-it gadget or invention that changes our lives. Grab a digital camera. Your task today is to take ten photos of ten things you consider to be great inventions. It's your opinion, so if you think it's great, capture it. Where's that back scratcher?

Was That Jeff or Did a Car Just Backfire?

They say that people who have lost one of their senses have increased awareness in the others. People who have lost their sight hear things those with sight don't hear. They become aware of their surroundings in a way others do not. Today, we're going to spend a little time becoming aware of our surroundings in a different way. For ten minutes straight, write down every single sound you hear. Don't look around; just look at the paper, or close your eyes, but write down each sound you hear. You might be surprised at what you pick up when you're paying attention.

where'd the cork go?

You just got a new client. *Hooray!* He has a special request that should take you all night to complete. Boo. Ahhh.... the life of a freelancing bottle designer. Your new client has a new "spirit," and he's asked you to create the craziest bottle shape ever known to retail spirit aisles everywhere. The only restriction is that it has to be able to fit on the shelf with the other bottles. *He wants people to remember his bottle, so it has to be unique.* He doesn't care how much it costs to create the bottle, only that it's the most unique ever created. Raise a glass to hoping the shine inside is half as good as the packaging!

Play Ball!

It's a wonderful day out here at the very first National Kickball League game. But where are the players? And the teams? By george, they haven't been named yet! Holy cow! Guess that means YOU will have to be the commissioner and name the cities and the teams. The NKL is an eight-team league, so create eight teams based in eight cities. You'll have to give them their team names as well. Choose names based on city or state highlights, kickball jargon or even names that simply would look good on the uniforms. You could even design the logos! Now go boot the ceremonial first roll.

You Mean There Really Is Truth in Advertising?

Advertising, by and large, has stretched the truth over the years to sell products. Not every product is truly the best. And not every product will perform the way it is represented. This we all know. But what if advertising told the truth? The late actor Dudley Moore made a comedy called Crazy People *that explored that very thought. Your task today is to create some truth in advertising. Choose three major car manufacturers, then choose one vehicle from each manufacturer. Write down your "truth in advertising" headline for each vehicle by creating a headline that, for once, actually communicates to the consumer what the vehicle really represents. When you're done, go rent* Crazy People.

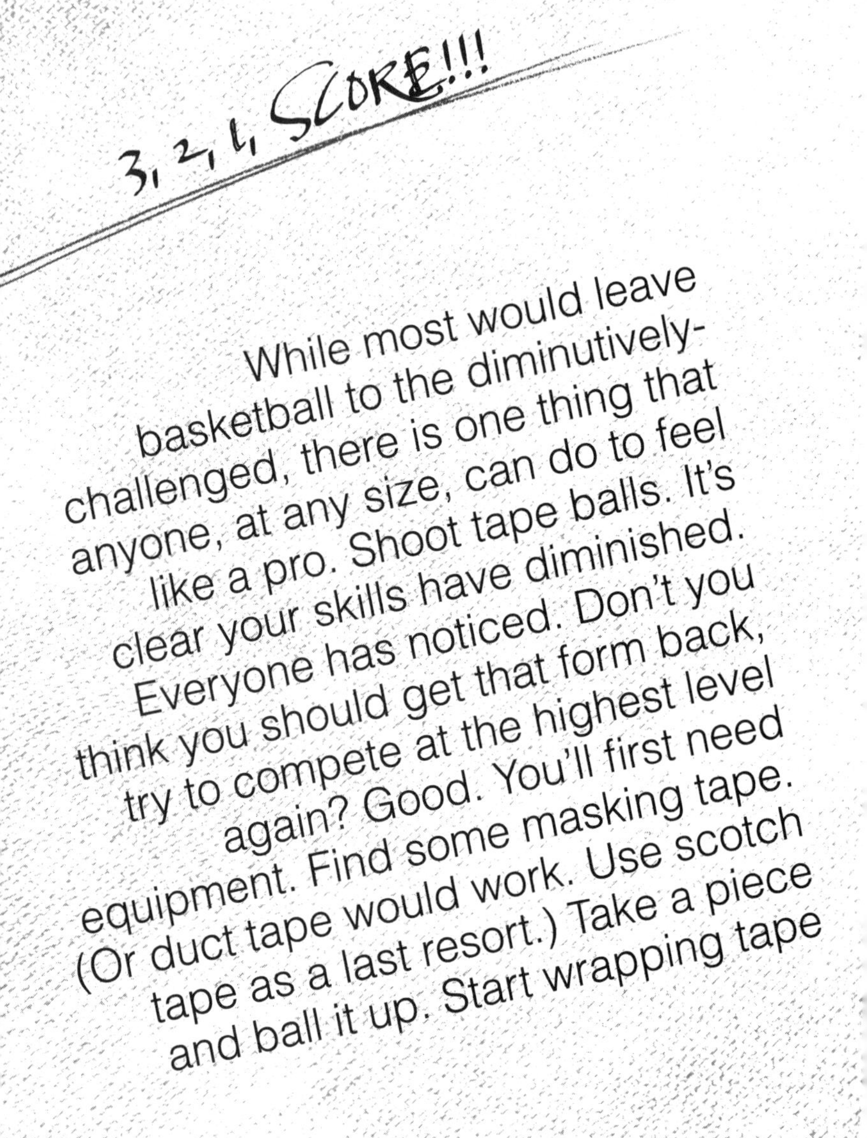

3, 2, 1, SCORE!!!

While most would leave basketball to the diminutively-challenged, there is one thing that anyone, at any size, can do to feel like a pro. Shoot tape balls. It's clear your skills have diminished. Everyone has noticed. Don't you think you should get that form back, try to compete at the highest level again? Good. You'll first need equipment. Find some masking tape. (Or duct tape would work. Use scotch tape as a last resort.) Take a piece and ball it up. Start wrapping tape around the ball until you have a ball about the size of an apple. Take a wastepaper basket and put it in an area that has at least twenty feet of space in one direction. Put a piece of tape on the ground five feet away from the basket. Then repeat this at ten feet, fifteen feet and twenty feet. The goal is to make one shot from all four spots on the floor consecutively. If you make the five foot shot, then move to the ten. If you miss the ten, you have to start back at five. Bombs away!

G.I. ...Douglas?

Almost everyone has had an interaction with an action figure at some point in their childhood… and maybe adulthood! Whether it's Barbie or G.I. Joe or Star Wars, action figures bring out the kid in all of us. Or at least they once did. We don't play with action figures much any more (or do we?) We all dreamed of what it would be like to actually be that hero or princess. We doubt the action figure ever wondered what it would be like to be us, but we're going to find out! Your challenge today is to create an action figure… of yourself. What kind of toy are you? How big are you? What does your packaging look like? Imagine you're on a store shelf and you have to convince a wandering child to run it back to mommy and convince her she really, really wants you. Sketch out the package, include accessories if you like, or just write out the marketing slogan and packaging hooks for your action figure!

INTERVIEW
WITH
VON
GLITSCHKA

What is "texture exploring?" Who would be described as a **"serial design killer?"** What constitutes a "doodle fanatic?" These questions, and many more, can be found in the brain of designer and illustrator Von Glitschka. Author of the "Bad Design Kills" movement (www.baddesignkills.com) and the Doodle Archive, Von knows a thing or two about creativity and idea generation. ***He even knows a thing or two about finding good help! "I'm a doodle fanatic," Von starts. "I keep sketchpads everywhere with me. I doodle wherever I'm at.*** And the thing is, I don't just toss them—I save literally every doodle I do. I have an envelope that I shove them in, and once that gets full I usually pay my daughter to paste them all up for me on 8.5 x 11 sheets of paper, and then I put them in plastic sleeves and then in a binder. So I have a doodle binder. **When the days come that I don't feel like drawing, I'll just pick up my doodle binder and start flipping though it and it'll kind of kick-start my creative process.**

If you can harvest your creative ideas and concepts when they're flowing and somehow document them, you'll be able to refer back to them when you need them. **I keep a little voice recorder in my car** so when I'm driving—and there's been times I remember seeing a sign or design or something, and I saw the negative space in the letters of the sign and I thought, 'Wow, that kind of forms a cool shape. That's a cool idea if I ever needed a logo mark like that'—I record it on my voice recorder, and when I get home I have a notepad and I log it in there. I keep track of those and save them for future projects."

Another method Von uses to harvest creative ideas is the concept of ***"texture exploring."*** "For as long as I can remember," Von says, "I've always enjoyed photography. When I was in art school, I would drive around with my camera and go out into the country and just look for cool, weatherized textures. I started doing this again about three years ago.

Digital photography has made it great to take these shots, come back to the studio and really create something organic out of them."

Von is also a big believer in doing creative work solely for the personal growth and enjoyment of the creator, without the monetary compensation or restrictions of a client. ***"I worked with in-house marketing departments, and I ran into the inevitable corporate policy. We called the people in marketing 'serial design killers.'*** It was difficult to stay true to my own design convention, but it's vitally important to do so. It's a balance. That's why I encourage young designers and creatives to create stuff just for themselves as well. A lot of people look at my work and they ask me who I did it for, and I say that I just do it for myself. I did it because it was fun! I didn't have to have a reason. I do this, otherwise I feel like I'm not pushing myself and I'm not growing as a designer. For instance, I just did an illustration of an owl a while ago, and the only reason I did it is because I saw a nature show on TV one night and they had this thing on baby owls. They were showing all these close-ups of the owls and I just thought I wanted to try to illustrate an owl. Not for a client or for any monetary profit, just for my own personal growth."

It seems if we desire to grow as creatives, we all need to find our baby owl once in a while.

Von Glitschka
Glitschka Studios
www.vonglitschka.com

Batteries Not Included

It seems everything has a starter kit. From poker to guitars to video games, if you're just starting out and you want all the necessary things you'll need to begin, there's a starter kit available. Too bad someone couldn't have left us a creative starter kit when we first started our jobs. It's time to become that someone. Your challenge today is to create a starter kit for your job. Create something to give to anyone starting in your occupation, or a starter kit for someone just beginning at your place of employment. Include a "Quick Glance" instruction sheet, something to give them the essential advice to succeed right away. Don't feel the need to make an actual box (unless you want to!), just write down what would be in the box, or sketch the starter kit on sketch paper. What would you want to have known when you started?

Ah, Go Fly a Kite

When's the last time you flew a kite? That long ago, huh? Let's test your memory: When was the last time you MADE a kite? You mean they had paper back then? Wow! Well, tomorrow, if someone asks you that question, you can proudly answer, "Why, just yesterday!" Your task today is to make a kite out of only the materials you have at your disposal right now. It can be as big or small as you like. The only stipulation is you HAVE to try and fly it when your done. Who makes a kite and doesn't fly it? ***Sheesh!***

Bland No Longer

The garden-variety orange traffic cone has been the universal symbol of "go away from here" for years. When otherwise friendly, outgoing people see an area where multiple orange traffic cones have gathered, they go the other direction, avoiding any contact with the cones. This has obviously led to a generation of orange traffic cone exclusion mindsets, dejected and inconsolable orange traffic cones taking their own cone lives on many occasions. In honor of your newfound hopeful desire to help change the cycle of cone abuse, your task today is to redesign or decorate the orange traffic cone to make it more inviting, to make people want to hang around cones once again. Think of it as "Extreme Makeover: Orange Traffic Cone Edition."

How Big Is A Bread Basket?

Recognizing relative size or distance is an underrated skill. The late Chick Hearn, long-time play-by-play broadcaster for the Los Angeles Lakers, was the king at being able to identify, from a country mile away, how far any shot attempt was from the basket. Your task today is to find the Chick Hearn in you. Grab a digital camera and take one picture of an object that satisfies each of the following criteria:

Is bigger than a coffee cup but smaller than a dinner plate.
Is smaller than a cat but bigger than a kitten.
Is bigger than a baseball but smaller than a football.
Is smaller than a car but bigger than a bicycle.
Is bigger than letter size but smaller than tabloid size.

Only take one picture for each criterion. Choose the objects by relative size only, not actual size.

I Can't Find "Downsizing"

Children's activity books have long carried many different kinds of word games. One of the most common is the word find. In a matrix of letters are buried a number of words that one must find, either horizontally, vertically, diagonally or even backwards. Your task today is to create a word find of your very own. You can start with as many letters across or down as you like. If you're searching for a good starting point, start with fifteen across and fifteen down. The first step is to choose a subject for your words, something they all have in common. Choose that subject from one of the choices below:

Your place of employment
Words that describe your family members
Animals that would make terrible pets
Things that smell foul
Last names of movie stars we'd rather not see anymore
The worst sports franchises in history
Font names
Nasty foods

Create at least ten words that belong in the category of your choice. Either use graph paper or draw out your fifteen by fifteen grid on a regular piece of paper, then start dropping in the words you created. Go vertically, both up and down, and horizontally, both forwards and backwards. Even throw in a couple on diagonals if the letters match up. Then fill in the remaining letters to complete your word find. Give it to a friend when you're done. If you chose "Things that smell foul," just make sure he's not in it!

Go Fighting Brain Men!

Every school has a mascot, the character that they stand behind as their own. From Eagles to Trojans to Conquistadors to Artists, every team has a physical representation of school spirit. Once we graduate, we're thrown out into the cold, cruel corporate world without an affiliation. That needs to change. Your task today is simple: Create your company mascot. It can be whatever entity you'd stand behind. The only restriction is it should go well with the chant **"Here we go, (insert your new mascot here), here we go! (clap, clap)"**

My Business Helmet Keeps Falling over My Eyes

From football to warfare to bikers, helmets have protected the domes of millions of people. Designed to deflect mortal wounds from reaching our skulls, we have relied on helmets to not only protect, but to communicate. Vikings wore helmets with horns attached in order to frighten and intimidate the enemy. Bikers have painted symbols and logos on their helmets for years, and football players have put notches on their helmets to signify certain goals reached. But the average joe doesn't really need to wear a helmet. The creative community is rarely in danger of striking death blows to one another's heads (although the thought has crossed our minds from time to time). Your task today is to create the helmet design for each of the following groups of people:

Hip Hop Artists
Ping Pong Players
Women Who Drink Tea
Business Executives
Librarians

Consider how that person would use the helmet, and what improvements you could make to allow more multi-sensory use out of the helmet. Strap it up!

You're Walking On My Line

There's an age-old adage that says **"A bad day golfing is better than a good day working."** Sometimes, you just have to find the silver lining. It's safe to say that in the absence of a full round of real golf, three holes of office golf will have to do. Your first task is to make a club. In the spirit of keeping everyone in the office safe from misguided drives, let's stick with just a putter. You have to find something to make into a putter, including creating the head of the putter. If you don't have any real golf balls around (who wouldn't?!) you can make tape balls with masking or duct tape. Now, all you need is the course. Spec out some space, either down hallways or in o p e n areas, where you can create your three-hole course. Using obstacles as hazards, create a putting course by creating the tee box with tape on the floor, and the flag by rolling up paper and taping it vertically to the floor. You can even create the flags if you like. Fore!

Do I Use Ballpoint or Felt Tip on the Inside of My Eyelids?

Sports radio talk show host Jim Rome once said "If you ain't cheatin', you ain't tryin'." While those in the spirit of fair play might disagree, its clear that many have taken the statement to heart, inventing extremely creative ways to cheat. Your task today is to join them. Not by cheating, but by thinking. Write down your top ten ways to cheat on a written exam. This is all hypothetical, of course. Isn't it?

Bachelor Number Three...

Before the bevy of dating reality shows, there was simply *The Dating Game*. One bachelorette, three eligible bachelors, a couple unique questions and a slew of creative answers. Regardless of your gender, your task today is to put yourself in the role of the eligible bachelors and come up with the best "Dating Game" answers to the following bachelorette questions:

If we were playing together at a park, what play park gym equipment would you want to play on first and why?

If there was a famous person in history who best represents your style, what person would that be and why?

If you and I went to dinner, but we only had $10 between us to spend, where would you take me?

If you were going to describe yourself as an instrument, what would it be and why?

Remember, you're trying to set yourself apart from the other two contestants, so come up with the answer that will make you unique and memorable!

I Think That Florist is a Total "H"

Letter forms have a design and style all their own. They are unique in shape, presentation and carry individualistic qualities that can be translated as mood in the right application. For instance, the difference between a "V" and an "O" is substantial, as the "V" is more violent and sharp, while the "O" is softer and more easy going. Your task today is to define the following people as letters, and explain why:

A serial killer
The first "John" you think of
A stunt man or woman
A plumber
The president of a company
A drill sargeant
A junior high gym teacher
Your boss

I'm For It... Wait... I Mean, I'm Against It

Everyone has an opinion. Today, you're going to make your opinion known, but in an abstract way. You're going to create a graphic that represents your opinion on one of the following charged topics:

Cigarettes
Welfare Checks
Guns
Birth Control
Vegetarianism

Choose one of the topics above, then choose a stance, either for or against it. Your task is to create an advertising graphic for your stance on the chosen topic. The twist is that you can only use the object in question. For instance, if you chose cigarettes, you can only use images of cigarettes in your graphic, no words and no outside elements. You can use more than one of the objects, and you can use them in any way you wish. Your layout can be complex or simple, but the elements that make up your graphic can only be of the object in question. The result should represent your stance on the topic.

Are Mom's Cookies an "X" or an "O"?

It's not difficult to visualize smells or sounds. Putting an image to the smell of a rose or the sound of an airplane isn't brain surgery, because we know what those objects look like. But what if we couldn't use the picture in our minds? What if we had to represent those senses visually using only abstract imagery? Your task today is to express the following sensory items visually using only the graphic symbols X or O.

The smell of poopy diapers
The sound of glass breaking
The sound of rain
The smell of a Christmas tree
The sound of a sneeze

Create a graphic representation of each of those sense experiences. Use scale, weight, quantity, pattern, size, placement, etc. to communicate the abstract situation.

Blind Man's Bluff

Visual observation is often our keenest form of awareness, but we have four other senses that are equally available to recognize and document occurrences. Let's find out just how strong one of those senses is! Go to a place you know, a place that is familiar and relatively busy. Bring a friend with you. Have your friend blindfold you and hand you a digital camera. Now, using only your sense of hearing, take snapshots with the camera… of sounds. Don't worry about focus, or even if you're pointed in the exact right direction, just react to sounds and take pictures of them, or in their general direction. Take at least twenty shots. You'll be surprised at what you are able to observe sonically—and the photos might even be surprisingly interesting!

Denise Weyhrich, Orange, CA

Coca-Cowpie?

Some of the most powerful brands on the planet right now are soft drinks. The graphic qualities of the packaging are recognizable for just about every person alive. It makes you wonder what soft drink packaging would have been like in historical times? Ok, maybe you don't wonder that, but you're going to start today. Your challenge is to create the soft drink can of choice for any of the following historical eras:

Old West
Impressionist Painters
Prehistoric Times
Medieval Times
Futuristic

Create the name of the soft drink, its flavor, and what the front of the can would look like.

doodles

Perspective is a key ingredient of creative thought. Everyone has a different perspective on everything, even if that perspective is only slightly different. The following pages represent the proof of this truth. Each of the featured interviewees from this book were given the same starting point: a simple squiggle, shown on the right. Here's what they did with it…

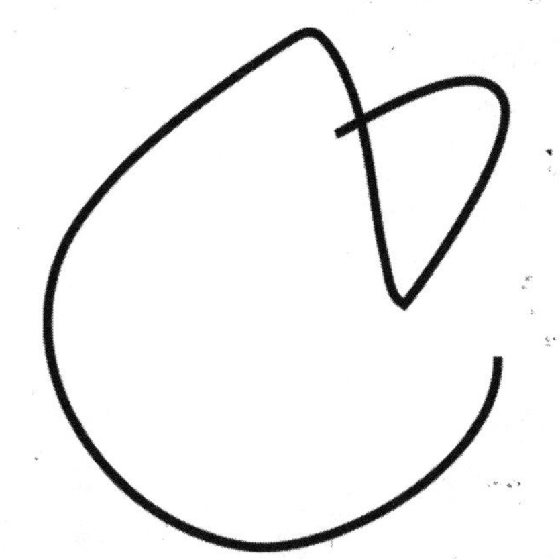

Use your own unique perspective to finish this drawing. Turn the paper to whatever angle you desire. There is no "right side up." Simply document what it is you see and finish the drawing using pencil, pen, crayons, inks, or whatever tool you'd like.

CAFFEINE CREATIVE MIND

EXERCISE 81

Perspective is one of creativity's most powerful allies.

In this exercise, you are asked to use your own unique perspective to finish this drawing. Turn the paper to whatever angle you desire, there is no "right side up." Simply document what it is you see and finish the drawing using pencil, pen, crayons, inks, whatever tool you'd like.

Please email your completed exercise to wendy@creativestretching.com or mail to:
Wendy Oldfield / Vekay Creative
1835 Newport Blvd. Ste A109-210
Costa Mesa, CA 92627

I DON'T MIND!

HEY, DO YOU MIND?

UNDERMINED

NEVER MIND

Denise Weyhrich

Kevin Carroll

John Sayles
Sheree Clark
doodles • DOODLES • doodles • DOODLES • doodles • DO

SOME GIRLS ARE BIGGER THAN OTHERS
HERE IS IMMEDIATE COMFORT FOR YOU WITH
RUPTURE-EASER
NO FITTING REQUIRED
$3.95
RUPTURE-EASER
RUPTURE-EASER
RUPTURE-EASER
RUPTURE-EASER
RUPTURE-EASER
10 minutes sketching while watching a terrible Oscar Wilde adaptation.
I think it had Reese Witherspoon + Colin Firth in it – wife's selection – I swear!
Paint etc. – done in 10 minutes while on the phone w/ clients in the office

John Foster

Mike Dietz
es • doodes • DOODLES • DOODLES • DOODLES • DOO

Von Glitschka

CAFFEINE FOR THE CREATIVE MIND
Exercise 81
Perspective is one of creativity's most powerful allies. In this exercise, you are asked to use your own unique perspective to finish this drawing. Turn the paper to whatever angle you desire, there is no "right side up." Simply document what it is you see and finish the drawing using pencil, pen, crayons, inks, whatever tool you'd like.
T MARKS

Terry Marks

Steve Morris
ODLES · doodles · DOODLES · doodes · DOODLES · D

WORLD'S
WORST
ARROW
Brian Sack

Top
06
Peleg Top
ES . DOODLES . Doodles . DOODLES . dOOdLes . Dood

Index

Design

Alohamobile	209
And It Still Staples	170
Bland No Longer	327
Box That Ferret, Please	146
Bugs Just Wanna Have Fun!	38
Coca-Cowpie?	339
Danger, Will Robinson, Danger!	41
Desks Ahoy!	309
Did You Get That License?	112
Do These Shorts Make My Line Look Big?	171
Does This Color Go With My Work Boots?	283
Does This Dress Make My Brain Look Fat?	181
Don't Put This on Your Hood, Though	182
Dude, C'mon!	49
Dude, Nice Koala Pinky!	73
Egg Drop Soup	46
Fore! Five! Watch Out!	124
G.I. ...Douglas?	320
Gnome, Gnome on the Range	69
Home Sweet Hobo Home	253
How About Dessert?	286
How Do You Draw "Music?"	157
How Many Ounces of Gold Do I Need to Park Here?	249
I Call Him "Upside Down Coffee Cup Man!"	254
I Call It Helveticaslon	196
I Have a Full House, Marketing Directors Over Production Thugs	260
I Wear My Sun-Survivor-Goggle-Glasses at Night	143
I Wouldn't Have Chosen Relish for the Carpet, But That's Just Me	185
I'm Flippin' Sweet!	301
I'm for It... Wait... I Mean I'm Against It	336
I'm Gonna Need a Bigger Fishbowl	188
I'm New and Improved!	126
Is Anyone Home?	28
Is It a Star?	276
Is That Chest of Drawers on a Dimmer?	248
Is That Hairnet Real?	288
It Looks Like a Scribble	257
It's Even Got Flaps!	131
Knock, Knock?	215

More Index

Let's Introduce You to Alex	153
Lick and Stick	225
Life In the Fast Lane!	164
Mine Has Five Colored Rings!	144
Mmmmm… Cardboard	130
My Astro-Toupee	70
My Business Helmet Keeps Falling Over My Eyes	331
My Totem Is Teetering	137
Our Janitor Doesn't Look Like That	115
Pablo Is Calling!	311
Pimp My Red Flyer	20
Poor Hamster… Never Had a Chance	194
Red and Blue Dogs	45
Retreat! Retreat!	302
Rock Star!	36
So Should I Stop Where I Am or Run?	129
"Stupid "K"	39
That Box Is Looking at Me	251
That Penguin Is Throwing Up on My Pants	166
There Is Always a Better Way	93
Three Things	83
Top Dog	160
Trick or Pantone Book?	205
Tweety Would Freak	204
Wanna Play Some Mini Desk Volleyball?	309
Wave 'Em Proud	183
What Is That Thing Dangling From Your Other Arm?	82
What Time Is It?	172
Where Was This 25 Years Ago?	98
Where'd You Get That Hot Chocolate, Dude?	238
Where's the Cork Go?	315
Why Can't I Have an Evil Lair, Too?	94
You Want an Acme What?	96

Idea Kindling

All Aboard!	236
An "E" Ticket Ride	133
And the Pitch… TOUCHDOWN!	116
Big Brother Is Not Only Watching, He's Brewing Cups of Coffee for You!	285
Black Eye Bart's a-Lookin' for Ya!	193

Surprise...Even More Index

Can Someone Show Me the Door? 136
Can You Feel the Love? 102
Did You Just Get Really, Really Mad at That Bank Robber? 208
Does That Come In Suede? 220
Don't Push That Button! 132
Et Tu, Rombus 3000? 110
Excuse Me, Your Three o'Clock Is Here 103
Go Fighting Brain Men! 330
Go Joe! 241
Hold On, I'm Folding My Quarter 80
I Actually Have a Need for a Hacksaw at My Studio 23
I Already Have That One! 147
I Can't Find the Surprise! 140
I Could Have Sworn That Sign Means "Walk Stiffly" 27
I'll Have the BBQ Rack of Vader Please! 221
I'll Take the Double Raptor Meal Deal Please 138
I'll Take the Next Catapult, Thanks 175
Is That a SuperSlushee Monument Built Out of Wieners? 239
Is That a Tailpipe, or Are You Just Happy to See Me? 227
It Keeps Things Hot and Cold! 158
It's Better Than Cleaning It! 247
Mmmm... Lincoln Logs 250
My Guard Rail Keeps Blocking the Scanner 255
My New Shoes Are Stuck In the ATM 168
Nice Hood Ornament! 106
One Meeelyun Daaaahhllers! 300
Pimp My Catapult! 117
Prehistoric Voicemail? 109
Sorry, Charlie 141
Superman's Not Home Right Now 154
Survival of the Fittest 92
Survivor: Madison Avenue 232
Tag, You're It! 305
Take a Seat 81
The Pet Rock Just Got Booted 174
The Ultimate Desk 43
What an Odd Place for a Totem Pole 222
White or Wheat? 108

What's an Index Anyway?

Photography

Blind Man's Bluff	338
Circular Heaven	26
Cool Vanishing Point!	299
Creatures of Habit	266
Doesn't Anyone Wear Yellow Anymore?	263
Drats	218
Dude, Feel Free to Pop a Mint	275
Good Fences Make Good Neighbors	62
Have You Ever Noticed That Before?	308
How Big Is a Bread Basket?	328
How Could I Live Without My Combination Hot Dog Cooker and Bun Warmer?	313
How Do You Get Your Lips Way Up There?	284
How Do You Photograph Smelly?	197
How'd That Get There?	21
I Changed That… I Think	280
I Knew That Xylophone Would Come In Handy One Day	258
If You Cross Your Eyes Like That, They'll Stay That Way	95
Is My Hair OK?	206
Is That a Paisley Screensaver?	291
Mini-It!	277
Sharpie; Shirt Pocket; Laundry Bill	77
That Looks Just Like Nothing!	104
What Does SHE Over THERE Have to Do With THAT?	187
Where Is That "Q" I've Been Saving?	48

Play

3, 2, 1… Score!!!	318
Ah, Go Fly a Kite	326
And Your Name Was…?	37
Did He Just Tell Me to Steal Third or Is His Nose Running?	127
Fire In the Hole!	262
High Fructose Corn Syrup Is Not a Banned Substance	24
I Make a Terrible Clown	256
If You Want to See Your Beloved Pencil Sharpener Alive…	267
It's Good to See a Happy Potato	240
It's Up, and It's Good!	264
Para-Military… Pens?	111
Shhhh. I'm Hunting Wabbits	63
Shoot! I Left the Ten Trophy Again!	216

Another Page of Index

Sure Beats Hand Puppets 261
The Wright Bros. Would Be Proud! 292
We Got the Beat! 192
What's a "Dot-Com?" 75
You're Fired! 184
You're Walking on My Line 332

Problem Solving

Can You Get Curds at the Deli Down the Street? 114
HEY! She Has My Hairdo! 274
How Do I Get Ink Off My Desk Again? 156
How Do I Make a Round Chimney? 231
How Do You Say "Red" In Caveman? 128
I Can't Hear You, I'm Screaming 312
I Knew I Should Have Saved That Copy of Ice Fishing Illustrated 282
I Never Knew a Pencil Sharpener Could Be So Deep 246
I Think That Florist Is a Total "H" 335
I Was Told There'd Be No Math 67
Are Mom's Cookies an "X" or an "O?" 337
Is That for a Dog Food Company? 269
Is This How Milton and Bradley Started? 169
Is That How They Made the Pyramids? 51
That Guy Is the Shape of a Caslon "R," Huh? 65
The Love Bug Returns! 35
This Exercise Puts So Much Pressure on Me… HEY! 25
Tick, Tick, Tick, Tick, Boom! 74
We Have So Much In Common! 281
Where's That Copy of Emotions Illustrated? 173

Writing

A Buffalo Would Definitely Destroy an Eagle In a Fight 268
A Little Dab'll Do Ya! 167
Agency Oz 100
And Then He Said… 234
Bachelor Number Three… 334
Back In My Day, the Fans Didn't Have Lasers 155
Balder-what? 293
Batteries Not Included 325
Can Anyone Direct Me to the Perfume Aisle? 85
Debate This! 289

Oh Boy, Even Another Index Page

Defend Yourself! 99
Did That Guy Just Say "Shucks?" 306
Do I Use Ballpoint or Felt Tip on the Inside of My Eyelids? 333
Don't Underestimate the Power of Example! 47
EXTRA, EXTRA! Read All About It! 290
For Sale 310
Haiku-a-Gogo! 265
Have a Nice Day! 224
Hi, I'm Fido 298
Holy Nightmares, Batman! 107
How Do You Sell "And?" 278
I Can't Come In, I Have the Gout 200
I Can't Find "Downsizing" 329
I Can't Spell "Abnormal Martian" With Just Seven Characters! 201
I Didn't Know I Had It In Me 159
I Didn't Think She Could Eat All of That 139
I Don't Think They Make a Slushee That Big 303
I Know He'd Have a Book of Potions, Right? 76
I Never Knew So Much About a Pencil Sharpener 190
I Think It Needs More (Insert Noun Here) 122
I Think My Seven-Year-Old Could Beat Me In a Race 34
I'll Take a Double Scoop of Pay-Toilet, Please 113
In a Land Far, Far Away... 135
Is That a Diamond Studded Coffee Mug? 78
Is That a Fire Pole? 125
It's Sort of Like Volleyball, But With Joe as the Ball 64
Like, Ummmm... I Mean, It's Like... 202
Mirror, Mirror on the Desk 101
My Words Caught a Fly 66
No Rules! 72
Oh No, They Didn't! 219
Oh, Say Can You Peep? 233
Once Upon a Tune 68
Play Ball! 316
Rest In Peace 145
Scott "Tired of Bein'" Poe Called for You 161
Shoot, I Pulled the Door Off Again! 162
Should Bees Wear Kneepads? 199
That's Great, Moses Is In Foul Trouble 226
That's Not the Words! 40

This Is The Last Index Page!

The "Million Dollar Idea" List.	50
The Envelope, Please	189
Twinkies Count as Two	198
Very Green	217
Was That Jeff or Did a Car Just Backfire?	314
Water and Air Are Cold	228
We're Gettin' Hitched!	207
We've Got Spirit, Yes We Do!	142
What Day Is It?	44
What Does "Melancholy" Look Like?	191
What Happens From Here?	235
What the Heck Is a Quince?	91
What's Next?	230
What's That Amazing Smell?	242
When Egg Noodles Die Young	252
Where'd They Get THAT?!	186
Where's This Going?	165
Would You Like Any Fillings or Gold Caps With THAT?	237
Yes, Doc, I Think I Broke My Pancreas Sleeping	203
You Got a "D" In Font Selection	84
You Mean There Really Is Truth In Advertising?	317

Contributors

Exercises
Derek Bender, Orlando, FL
Laura Barnes, Cary, NC
Sharon Figel, East Windsor, NJ
Alexandra Sokol, Los Angeles, CA
Callene Abernathy, Port Orchard, WA
Kevin Ehlinger, Avon, MN
Ashley Lang, Portland, OR
Kate Dow, Des Moines, IA
Rob Morgan, Costa Mesa, CA
Lauren Goldberg, Chicago, IL
Linda Lauro-Lazin, New York, NY
Jonathon Redman, Roachdale, IN
Marc Swarbrick, Annesley Woodhouse, Nottinghamshire, England
Misha Mace, Bellingham, WA
Denise Weyhrich, Orange, CA
Pattie Bacheldor, Atlanta, GA

Featured Interviews
Jeff Fisher, Jeff Fisher Logomotives, www.jfisherlogomotives.com
John Sayles, Sayles Graphic Design, www.saylesdesign.com
John Foster, Fuszion Collaborative, www.fuszion.com
Kevin Carroll, The Katalyst Consultancy, www.katalystconsultancy.com
Steven Morris, Morris! Communications, thinkfeelwork.com
Von Glitschka, Glitschka Studios, www.glitschka.com
Mike Dietz, Slappy Pictures, www.slappypictures.com
Denise Weyhrich, Seeds Fine Art Exhibitions, www.seedsfineart.org
Brian Sack, Banterist, www.banterist.com
Terry Marks, TMarks Design, www.tmarksdesign.com
Peleg Top, Top Design Studio, www.topdesign.com

I Tried Its
Jessica Southwick, Old Saybrook, CT
Margaret Minnis, Lake Forest, CA
Candace Gallant, Mount Horeb, WI
Eric Chimenti, Orange, CA
Mike Pierce, Los Alamitos, CA
Tamar Wallace, Boston, MA
Trevor Gerhard, San Clemente, CA
Julia Scannel, Napa, CA
John Kleinpeter, Irvine, CA
James Maciariello, Irvine, CA

More great titles from HOW Books!

Creative Sparks
An Index of 150+ Concepts, Images and Exercises to Ignite Your Design Ingenuity
by Jim Krause

This playful collection of rock-solid advice, thought-provoking concepts, and valuable exercises is sure to stimulate the creative, innovative thinking that designers need to do their jobs well. Anyone working in marketing or design will find inspiration and new ideas with this creative guide.

ISBN 13: 978-1-58180-438-6, ISBN: 1-58180-438-5, $24.99 pob, 312 p, #32635

Inspirability
40 Top Designers Speak Out About What Inspires
by Pash

Written and compiled by Pash, this book offers an original take on one of the most requested topics by graphic designers—how to stay inspired when working on a deadline. Interviews with 40 of today's top designers and insights into day-to-day inspiration make Inspirability a must-have tool for every graphic designer.

ISBN 13: 978-1-58180-555-0, ISBN: 1-58180-555-1, $34.99 hc, 240 p, #33011

IdeaSpotting
How to Find Your Next Great Idea
by Sam Harrison

Seasoned business pro Sam Harrison offers real and unique insight into the creative process, as well as exercises to help anyone generate viable business ideas. This book trains business people to step outside their daily routine to find their next great idea by encouraging spontaneity and exploration.

ISBN 13: 978-1-58180-800-1 ISBN: 1-58180-800-3, $14.99 pb, 256 p, #33478

These and other great HOW Books titles are available
at your local bookstore or from online suppliers.

www.howdesign.com